Collected Poems
1940–1990

Collected Poems 1940–1990
Maurice Lindsay

ABERDEEN UNIVERSITY PRESS
Member of Maxwell Macmillan Pergamon Publishing Corporation

First published 1990
Aberdeen University Press

© Maurice Lindsay 1990

The publisher acknowledges subsidy from the Scottish Arts Council
towards the publication of this volume.

British Library Cataloguing in Publication Data

Lindsay, Maurice *1918–*
   Collected poems 1940–1990
   I. Title
   821.912

   ISBN 0-08-040910 5

Printed in Great Britain by
Billing & Sons Ltd, Worcester

Contents

Introduction

An author's *Collected Poems* should contain all he thinks worth preserving. In 1979, Alexander Scott made a judicious selection of my work under the title *Collected Poems*. In a sense this, too, is a selection, but a final one since I have discarded much that no longer satisfies me. On the other hand, unlike some poets, I have no difficulty whatever in re-experiencing past impulses that led to the writing of many of my earlier poems. Having, in Burns' quaint phrase, 'commenced poet' during the early years of the 1939–45 war, I fell into the then fashionable habit of publishing pieces insufficiently revised, or treating of matters which I did not then have the necessary technical ability to realise. Many of these earlier poems have therefore undergone substantial later revision.

I have divided the book roughly into chronological sections, the sources of the poems being indicated in the section headings. Where poems have been revised, they have been included in the section to which the originals belong, but with the date of the revision indicated in the list of Contents. I do not wish any other versions than those included here to be reprinted in the future, for whatever purpose. The final section consists of a selection of my lighter verses, pieces with no other aim than to entertain.

I am indebted to many of my friends for advice and criticism where I had doubts, but above all to my old friend and fellow-poet, George Bruce, for his constructive and encouraging criticism and comment throughout the half-century of my creative activity.

I

Poems from *Perhaps To-morrow* (1941),
Predicament (1942), *No Crown for Laughter* (1943),
The Exiled Heart (1946)

London, September 1940

Helplessly the wavering searchlights probe
   where stuttering bombers fly:
each thud and flash their faceless pilots lob,
   anonymous numbers die,
shaking a length of protest from the ground:
   ack-ack guns chatter,
more distant heavies boom, and make resound
   the emptiness they batter.

Watching these beams meet in the cloudy blue
   of this unsummered night's
bewildered terror, foolishly, it's you
   who lingers in my sights,
eyes wide upon *Les Sylphides*. I remember
   you sitting at my side
through the uneasiness of that September
   when thought of peace died,
the sway of whiteness as the music dreamed
   what only music knows;
joy, more intense since it already seemed
   lost in our long-agos:
applause; the broken spell; cheer upon cheer
   for delicate civilisation,
as if the audience sensed that they'd been near
   some final consummation:
the heavy curtain tumbling from the ceiling;
   the glow of the house lights;
lifting a fur around your shoulders, feeling
   love must set all to rights:

helping you rise; the popping-back of your seat;
   a statue's marble stare;
your clinging little shudder as we met
   a coldly threatening air;
the newsboy hoarsely calling—*Hitler speaks;*
   the separating fear
of distance, blanched like powder on your cheeks
   at the mere thought of war . . .

Now it has happened. Searchlights take the sky,
and naked in another's arms you lie.

A Teacher of the Violin
(Camillo Ritter: Graz 1875—Helensburgh 1940)

Friend of my growing up, guide of my striving,
so much I'd hoped for lies within your grave;
though there's no answer to such skill's undoing,
I'm left at least the influence you gave.

Something must be for saving, since fresh grief
tempers the mind with time to make us wise
enough to know that reason needs belief
if doubts are not to sleep with sightless eyes.

Watching you sink to your adopted earth,
I leave you silence; a soldier now, my fate
marshalled to enfilade the march of death
whose music's the cacophony of hate.

Central Station, Glasgow: December, 1939

Wheel-deep in platform, steaming engines wait
the staring clock that signals red to green.
Pressed to his girl, the soldier's fondled dream
of daily touch, shared bed and kids, can't sate

the anguish of that torn-apart embrace
through which anonymous enemies mount their fire.
Heavy with packs and half-fulfilled desire,
each gazes on a troubled upturned face;

as if the close-up memory of down
on cheek, the curve of lip or breast, or smell
of womanliness, might one day rise to spell
some final courage, empty of renown.

Late carriage doors get slammed. The brave disguise
the women wear like make-up cracks to pain
as hastily the men fall silent or repeat again
assurance doomed to fade with their goodbyes.

O God of battle, steeling soldiers' hearts. . . .

A whistle blows, another train departs.

Home on Leave

The train from London breathes up the Northern line,
dead on time when the rise of the Westmoreland fells
folds back her speed till her boiler's forced to pant
great gasps of steam over Shap; past mountain rills

white with a stumbled fall of energy;
past sloping sheep and loosely-straggled walls
reaching to hold the edge of scree and sky
together, where low rains have stripped the hills.

Home-on-leave, home-on-leave, the wheels go dicketty-dack,
as the engine shrieks at the summit and shakes itself free;
and I wonder where in the breadth of fourteen days
I'll find the year-lost self that was pre-war me.

The acrid soot that clung to the station's arch
hangs thicker; the girl whose eyes flash a quick embrace
half-looks beyond the edge of her welcoming
as if mine were no longer the only close-up face.

I lounge in the clothes that fitted me once with ease,
strange as worn attitudes; the constraints of war
have sized me out of whatever I thought I was
in a blur of distance neither near nor far.

Beside the chafering troop-trains, severed wives
hug men beyond the reach of what either knows;
the girl who swore she'd wait lets a stranger go
to his own sufficiency as the whistle blows.

The train to London gulps down the Southern line,
past terraced houses, drabness crazily rent
by jig-saw bombs, the unconsecrated pile
of a silenced church, to fields with barbed-wire bent
rehearsing conflict, mile after broken mile.

Battle Drill

You whom I have so often watched
playing the simple acts of living,
reading a letter from home, or laying
questions to puzzle a favourite cat;

you for whom I have so much love
that waking hours have hung on my heart,
are marbled as the maelstrom lowers
in a white attitude of hate.

Now, as I watch a ritualled killing
guide the slow movements of your thighs,
history's triumphs cannot hide
these heavy pains of emptied love.

Crawling, you crush the peering lilies
stretching red eyes of slow surprise,
dreaming of seed, not the sharp treachery
that traps a man into reaping lives.

Oh, but the lilies cannot answer
tears, or the questioned minute's grief!
Spring is still happy, though my years
are narrowed as I watch you move.

The Trigger

Only the trigger keeps him apart from Death;
to join their hands, I simply move my finger
and a bullet will pierce a hole in my enemy's breath.

Perhaps his breath would leak from him slowly, linger
a little, like air from a limply deflating balloon,
or the silence trailing the voice of a passionate singer,

and he would be still half-man, like the white morning moon
fading fainter under a blue cloth sky,
the end of living a longed-for, cursed-at boon;,

till on a cushion of memories he would lie—
the shape of his young wife's mouth, his child's thin hair:
how living emptied when one came to die!

Or it might all be over quickly, an affair
of absolute destruction; the heart ripped
or the brain scattered, quietly unaware.

And yet, if only my curling finger slipped
another would shake Death's casual welcoming hand
and follow on into his useless land;

a man who somehow is my enemy
would laugh and load again, and still be free.

The Exiled Heart

Two purple pigeons circle a London square
as darkness blurs and smudges the shadowless light
of a winter evening. I pause on the pavement and stare
at the restless flutter of wings as they gather flight,
like rustling silk, and move out to meet the night.

And my restless thoughts migrate to a Northern city —
fat pigeons stalking the dirty, cobbled quays,
where a sluggish river carries the cold self-pity
of those for whom life has never flowed with ease,
from a granite bridge to the green Atlantic seas:

the bristling, rough-haired texture of Scottish manners;
the jostling clatter of crowded shopping streets
where lumbering tramcars squeal as they take sharp corners:
the boozy smell from lounging pubs that cheats
the penniless drunkard's thirst with its stale deceits:

where my heart first jigged to the harsh and steady sorrow
of those for whom mostly the world is seldom glad,
who are dogged by the flat-heeled, footpad steps of tomorrow;
for whom hope is a dangerous drug, an expensive fad
of the distant rich, or the young and lovesick mad:

where chattering women in tearooms, swaddled with furs,
pass knife-edged gossip like cakes, and another's skirt
is unstitched with sharp words, and delicate, ladylike slurs
are slashed on the not-quite-nice or the over smart
till smoke to the eyes is a hazy, prickled hurt.

I remember Glasgow, where sordid and trivial breed
from the same indifferent father; his children side
with the mother whose sour breasts taught them first to feed
on her hot, caressing hates that sear and divide,
or swell the itching, distended bladder of pride.

Yet my guilty sneers are the tossed-down, beggar's penny
which the goaded heart throws out, in vain, to procure
the comfortable forgetfulness of the many
who lie in content's soft arms, and are safe and sure
in the fabled Grecian wanderers' lotus-lure;

who forget the sullen glare of the wet, grey skies,
and the lashing Northern wind that flicks the skin
like a whip, where poverty's dull and listless eyes
are pressed to the window, hearing the friendly din
of the party, watching the lights and laughter within.

But oh, I cannot forget! So I wait and wonder,
how long will the thinly dividing window hold,
how long will the dancing drown the terrible anger
of those, the unwanted, who peddle their grief in the cold,
wrapped in their own despair's thick and unkindly fold?

Yet evil is no pattern of places
varied, like terraces from town to town;
a city's charms and individual graces
are but the sculptor's bleak and basic stone,
the photographic face without a frown.

The wound is in this bewildered generation,
tossed on the swollen, analytic mood,
its compass-point no longer veneration
of that lost God who rewarded the simple and good,
vivid and real, now, only in childhood.

For we, the children of this uncertain age,
breathing its huge disasters and sad airs,
have seen that our warm, humanitarian rage
is impotent to soothe war's animal fears,
can never quell the lonely exile's tears.

So the heart, like a wounded seabird, hungers home
to muffled memories on faintly-beating wings
which once climbed over history's clouded foam
to that clear sky where each new hero flings
the careful stone that fades in slow, concentric rings.

Poem at Christmas

Tonight, a crisp air clings to the traveller's face,
sharpens quick diamonds set in city snow;
now, from this Northern land, I cross the space
between me and two thousand years ago,

where, in a stable, wind hustling the door,
a woman labours. Her distracted cries
startle the steamy oxen on the floor
staring at her with moist and curious eyes.

What puzzled thoughts were awkward Joseph's then,
hearing the cattle's hot, half-foetid breath
and the creaking rafters; seeing his Mary's pain
with more than ordinary fear and faith?

Did he picture stately processions through a crowd,
obeisance, jewels, the triumphant crown;
seasons and winds in their courses filled with the loud
glad truth that somehow the world would suddenly own?

Or was it all so much a personal thing—
how thin the straw that covered the cold, grey stone:
what it might do, this child his wife would bring
into the earth as his, that he'd not sown?

Likely his dreams were those of simple men,
hailing new birth to carry the sick years on,
learning always the need to begin again
as the slow candle of the breath burns down.

How could he guess, watching a lantern flame
flicker its quiet shadows on the wall,
stroking her hand, half-murmuring her name,
that centuries would centre on this stall;

movements and people, churches, towers rise,
vaunt their vainglory for the gentle sake
of One who came with healing in His eyes
to fishers by a Galilean lake:

that only His difficult birth could be wholly glad,
the world, as always, trundle its selfish way;
though a few would listen, most would consider Him mad,
and all would deny His love at the end of the day?

As I reach in my fancy towards that far-away scene,
share the wild joy that to shepherds a white star brought,
more than the earth's blind turning has come between
me and that wondrous babe three wise men sought;

more than clean time: the accretions of history
have piled their lumber on the accepting heart,
Death's unjust litter clogged the mystery,
so that the mind can no longer see it apart

from the tragic human act; the unkempt fears
of poverty, lean hunger's cancerous ache,
the gash of unnatural loss, and the frozen tears
of wars that have broken pity over the rack.

To some, it is mostly an unbelievable story—
a sweet-faced Italian madonna in gold and blue,
a naked babe at her breast, in a halo of glory—
with a half-smothered hope that still it might all prove true,

that over the newspapers' clamoured advance or retreat
the long-ago angels' *et in terra pax*
would fall as softly as snow on this Glasgow street,
like sleep on a child, and the straining would relax.

To-night, as I turn to the Christmas-cracker glow,
the party songs, gay lights and the yellow sherry
pledging the usual toast that the ways we go
will be hedged with success, and all our days be merry,

my faith, like wine in a half-filled, uncorked bottle
has lost its taste, gone bitter and flat and thin.
Nothing I do will strengthen the flavour a little;
no gesture of mine can pour a new wine in.

So I watch the spectrum that plays on the delicate glass
you hold to the light, my darling; and looking at you
I pray that whatever the future may bring to pass
that will hurt or please or maim, we may always be true

to ourselves and each other; to those who have suffered defeat
and are broken and weak, for whom love is an angry swan,
its beauty shedded, hoarse terror craning its beak,
attacking the cloud-white dream it once sailed upon.

For love is the only faith that is certain and sure,
the only belief that follows no guideless star,
leading the vagrant heart to that stable door
and the symbolled birth no staleness can ever mar.

The Sudden Picture
(for Joyce)

My days are stained with people, purposeless
and restless as the heart of this hurt city;
hopes geared like watches, darted troutlike fears,
and the exquisite paraphernalia of self-pity.

Walking in these white, half-frightened streets,
I remember you, leaning against a wind from the Tay;
the smile your eyes launched into loveliness
that drowned the careful words I meant to say.

I might have told you just the usual stories
each first new lover weaves into a name;
held you above the well-applauded glories,
or wrapped you in a personal dream of fame.

But I said nothing; for the sudden picture
you made against a light blown from the sea
mocked war's unnatural, accidental virtue
and meant far more than Stalingrad for me.

Now all the roads of Europe lead to horror,
time cannot heal Cassino's fountained stones;
beneath the gag of darkness, millions cower
in menaced, dingy, still unbattered homes.

They are gashed with the same guilt, friend and enemy,
a wound reeks round their striving circled years:
the future mirrors back reversed deceptions,
tomorrow floats on history's stale tears.

My darling, since the words I never uttered
were more than guns' mad gestures, more than death's
advances over towns that men have shattered,
I send you love, and with it all my faith.

To Hugh MacDiarmid

The English see you as an angry eagle
who tears at them with sharp and furious claws:
a mad, persuasive Gael who would inveigle
the Celts to raise their long-abandoned cause.

Sometimes they see you set in Highland weather,
red glens of shaggy cattle, a bleak moor
where game-birds flutter from the fading heather,
dark-scented pine-woods laced with pointed spoor.

Or like the island clansman in the posters,
meeting the steamer once or twice a day;
or fishing with dour crofters for blue lobsters
to fill the creel-pots anchored in the bay.

They think that in your stern and rocky language
you catch the scudding Hebridean spray;
that words like sparks are only cast to furbish
the violent moods of Scottish history.

Your kilt, and all your gestures of romancing
are quaint; but oh! it's late into the day
to turn aside the leisurely advancing
of England on her humanistic way.

And so they smile with unconcerned indulgence,
pay tribute to the temper of your thought,
admire your passion's vigorous effulgence,
but not the cause for which you lived and fought.

Foreigners see our country veiled in romance,
a land where savages robbed and roved in clans;
our people, slow, unwilling to advance,
soft-spoken ghillies, shooting hands
who labour to provide the Autumn sport
of English lairds, but never understand
the conscious English joke or the stock retort.

You have put that contemptuous nonsense back in its place,
and are no longer concerned with the rotting shielings,
the dreary, crumbling dust of a vanished race;
but with those steady hands and hearts that are willing
to cultivate the grey and desolate space
two hundred empty years have left behind;
the drizzling littleness of the Scottish mind.

For you are not contained by the edge of an age,
easing the sharp, contemporary itch
with a trumped-up tag or a newly polished adage
for the anxious eyes that stare at their own last ditch;
but one who, on Time's only mountainside,
searches the clouds for where the heavens divide.

From Scotland's 'Who Was Who'

I JOCK, THE LAIRD'S BROTHER

Strutting across the red moors of his memory, Jock, the Laird's
    brother,
tingling, tweedy bagpipe trousers, whisky map-veined face,
under his arm a leering gun, the image of his father,
the skirling tradition of fishes and pheasants, the ownership of
    space;

the purple, peopleless moors of Scotland where povery seeds in the
    ground,
and love turns grey as the ashy, prickled, bleak-burned skeletoned
    heather,
where sleek guns splutter their patter in August, and gasping
    grouse are found
on the noses of snuffling dogs, and the hills are always the talk of
    weather.

Once, he was keeper of animals claimed from God to be owned by
    a Scottish lord;
once, he patrolled the edge of forests, a poacher's pleasure his full
    despair;
now, he is grown the villagers' measure with his regular walks, an
    old man, absurd,
with the look of one who's been left behind by thoughts that were
    never there.

II THE NEW LAIRD

One day the old laird trembled, pinched and lean,
a leaf unsapped for moulding back to earth,
taking some comfort in his last extreme
young Jock still lived to heir his troubled hearth.

So Jock moved in, an ageing country-dweller,
beneath the mournful stare of glass-eyed stags,
to mortgaged foost, a much-depleted cellar   mould caused by
and the library of well-recorded 'bags'.   dampness and disuse

Now spindle-shanked, each day he greets relations
empanelled on the proud baronial walls,
willing the family's mottoed exhortations
upon him as he echoes through their halls.

But nothing in these cracked and postured features
frowning reproof or fixed in spent command,
shows that they know what's happened to the servants,
or why he's had to part with half their land.

So, hail or shine, he tames the shrinking heather,
potting whatever flies or leaps or slinks,
then grumbles to his fire of worsening weather
and laces his bewilderment with drinks.

III   CELIA, THE WIFE O THE LAIRD

Mrs Mackintosh, wi heather-mixture suit,
hauds oot frae Brechin in a black coupé:
we condescendan mien she gies a toot
an scatters sheep an fairmers frae her way.

We gracefu ease, she purrs alang the road,
jinkan roun corners, shearan aff the hedge,
content we smeddum that gat her sic a load
o whisky, meat an cigarettes for Reg.

Aside her, Pooh, her Pomeranian dug,
snuffles the air an stoiters roun the seat,
syne stretches oot upon the tartan rug
with twitchan nose fowr inches frae the meat.

Mountains and woods flow past her like a flick—
Charming, she thinks, the Scottish Rural Scene—
Wi artfu glances Pooh begins to lick
the paper whaur a pund o mince had been.

A line o cedars sweepan up a lawn,
an, hame again, the weekly journey's done.
The heather-mixture's crinkl't sit-upon
get oot an stretches like a yeastfu bun.

In green plus-fowrs and cheery Oxford cry,
Reggie comes amblan oot tae greet his wife.
Anither week the warld can whiffle by;
the laird's well-bieldit frae the blasts of life.

IV GENERAL WITHERS

The faded general with the antler knees
watches the Spring's offensive run;
follows close on the heels of summer
with double whisky and double gun.

Autumn lauds him with blood and feathers,
puffy tweeds on a crunching field;
sighted by monocle, deer and game-birds
fall from their ambience and yield.

Winter betrays him hot on the carpet
bidding advancing years disband;
time sneaks under the guard of bluster,
rattles the tumbler in his hand.

Death convenes its surprise Court Martial,
rips the glazed honours off the chest
of an out-manoeuvred map-bound hero;
the sentence, one he can't contest.

Outside, retainer Earth lies waiting;
waiting, as thirty years ago,
its master then a rich provider,
it waited on this general's biggest show.

II

Poems from *Hurlygush* (1948),
At the Wood's Edge (1950),
Ode for St Andrew's Night (1951),
The Exiled Heart (1959)

Hurlygush

The hurlygush and hallyoch o the watter   noise of water on stones
skinklan i the moveless simmer sun
harles aff the scaurie mountain wi a yatter   peels
that thru ten-thoosan centuries has run.

Wi cheek against the ash o wither't bracken
I ligg at peace and hear nae soun at aa   lie
but yonder hurlygush that canna slacken
thru time and space mak never-endan faa:

as if a volley o the soun had brocht me
doun tae the pool whaur timeless things begin,
and e'en this endless faa'in that had claucht me
wi ilka ither force was gether't in.

Whaup i the Raip

There's a whaup i the raip, the fairmer cried   bird in the corn
as the winnock gaed snick-snack;
the deil it's a loon I niver could bide . . .
He rcishit upstairs lik ane gan wud,   dashed angrily/mad
an there, hauf-naked, his dochter stude,
    hacn tint whit she couldnae git back,   lost
    ay, tint whit she couldnae git back.

He rantit and ravit, cursed lassies wha grene,   are lustful
he cae'd her a slut an a reip,   trollop
but she smiled wi a faur-awa look in her een;
Why fash when there's neither revince nor   bother/reversal
                  remeid?   remedy
There's nocht ye can dae but tak tent o the deed,   note
    sae ye micht jist as weel haud your threep,   shut up
    ye micht jist as weel haud your threep!

A Penny for your Thoughts

A penny for your thochts, she cried,
   I'll no gie ony mair
for ocht that gars you luik sae white
   an lik a maukin stare!   hare

Thon's no the lift ahint you, lass
   nor ony ither thing
that kens the ticht skin o the warl',
   or kythes wi'in its ring.

The starns hae preened you tae the nicht,
   an derkness haps your face,
an tumblan frae your sides lik bluid
   faa entless lynns o space.   waterfalls

The centre o the universe
   bursts open lik a woun',
an whummlan lik a mountain burn   tumbling
   God's mind gaes brattlan doun—

O tak my hinny mou, she leuch,
   an baith my breists tae kiss,
syne in my airms there's nocht in yirth
   or Heaven'll seem amiss!

At the Cowal Games, Dunoon

Haveran, bletheran, yatteran folk   over-wordy
   thrang the streets roun the pier,   crowd
ilka Jeannie lays haud o her Jock
   an bangs her wey thru the steer.   pushes/crowd

There's tartan tammies an muckle blads   posters
   tae shaw the garb o the clans:
there's thistl't lassies an kiltit lads
   wi the emblems o fitba fans.

The whussle an jostle an rankringan din,
  the stour an the heat o the day
are suddentlie naethin, for aa are kin
  whan the thoosand pipers play.

As the skirlan soun drifts up tae the hills
  an spreids owre the skinklan sea,
there's fient a breist but gaes faster and fills   <small>not one</small>
  wi whit Scotland yince could be.

Yet afore the echo has cool't i the bluid,
  there's blawan o gee-gaws again,
an Scotland's back tae her doited mood
  o snichteran, sneet, hauf-men!

Bairnsangs

I SIMMER EFIRNOON

The milk's gane blinkit i the can,   <small>on the turn</small>
fish reeshles i the fryin-pan;
a spinnan-Jennie's threid-like knees
birse, till her prin-heid's i the bees,   <small>buzz</small>
  against the winnock-pane.

Oot i the foggit gairden shed
twa spiders speil ane clortit web;   <small>climb/dirty</small>
an jifflan jukes sloch roun the slyke   <small>shuffling/slouch</small>
afornens their ramshackle byke,
  mindan o eggs lang lain.

Ayont the yett, slow rowean swaws   <small>gate</small>
flodder the rocks and fill the gaws   <small>flood</small>
whaur sea-maws glink, or flick their een,
wi yalla beaks their feathers preen,
  and syne flee aff again.

II IN THE ENGINE-ROOM O THE PADDLE-STEAMER 'JEANIE DEANS'

Crankshafts and pistons chitter and slide
    their kelteran, glittie faces;   *shining/oily*
a lithe clanjamphrie o pooerfu pairts   *active assembly*
    aa ettlan tae shaw their paces.   *striving*

As I glower at the deeps o yon siller churm,
    like a preen tae a magnet haudan,
I canna see hoo the boat sails on
    as the outcome o aa this doddan.

Is it no sae with the bauch auld warld,
    whaur nane o us properly ken
the antran forces doddan aboot   *miscellaneous*
    that nevel the weird o men?   *shape/fate*

III INFINITY

Gin I was Betelgeuse
birlan awa up there
frae the first reid flichter o time
tae the end o evermair,
I wudna be lanesome, whiles,
for the stairns, the sun an the mune
'ud be whinneran, lik masel,   *spinning*
till the whang o the Lord wore dune.   *thong*

IV THE GUINEA-FOWL

Wi her speckit gray coatie
    pued owre her humph-back,
and her neb tae the groun,
    the guinea-fowl's 'Chack'
        girns aa roun the fairm;   *grumbles*
        but she means nae hairm.

For she's sic a queer shape,
   she maun baith soun crabbit   bad-tempered
an luik an auld wifie
    aye shochlan and wabbit.   shuffling
     If sic was your bane   lot
     would you no, whiles, complain?

V   THE-MAN-IN-THE-MUNE

The man-in-the-Mune's got cleik-i-the-back   rheumatism
an wullna come oot tae play.
He sits by himsel on a shimmer o Heaven   cross-bar
an hears whit the starnies say.

But his cheeks gae black, he purls his broo
an his auld heid shaks wi rage
thru the reengan cloods that jostle the earth
whan God's on the rampage.

VI   THE PARTAN

Ae crustit shell, two claws and een,
aucht legs growean oot o his shouthers:
he scrabbles owre the flair o the sea,
sae's you canna tell whaur neist he'll be,
for gin the wind but fluthers
you'll think it was aiblins a stane you've seen.
But gin it really is the partan,   crab
intae the sand he'll gae doun scartan!

                    scratching

VII   WILLIE WABSTER

Hae ye seen Willie Wabster,
   Willie Wabster, Willie Wabster?
He's weil-kent frae Scrabster
   tae yont the siller Tweed.

He scarts his fingers owre the lift,   scratches
   an sets the starns a-shoggin;
when thunner-cloods'll haurdly drift,
   he gies ilk yin a joggin.

An when the mune offends his sicht,
　he coosts it owre his shouther;
an whiles, tae snuff the sun's gowd licht,
　his winds begin tae fluther.

He gars come dingan on the toun
　the raindraps oot o Heaven,
draps frae his pooch an dangles doun
　in bauns, the colours seven.

Sma wunner that I'm aften scared,
　for I'm no certain whether
he's God Himsel, the warld's ae laird,
　or jist His clerk-o-weather!

VIII　A BAIRN'S PRAYER NICHT

The starns crack the lift　　　　　　　　　sky
　tae let licht in;
sae please may the holes
　let oot my sin.

IX　THE SPEUG

The speug's aye dressed in midden-claithes　　sparrow
　o doucelik, hamely broun;
he's unco blate an flees awa
　gin sprucer birds licht doun.

But when he's by his lane he cheeps
　a cheerfu kailyard sang,
syne perks his heid, and picks his breid,
　an hap-hap-haps alang.

X　BURN MUSIC

Murmell, murmell, murmell,
croodles the burn
as heid owre heels
its watters turn,

puan the blue-grass
that hings frae the shair,
an sheinan the stanes
o its clean cobbl't flair.

Brattle, brattle, brattle,
the wee lynn sings   water-fall
as tumblin frae craigs
the burn taks wings;

a fantice o faem   fantasy
it loups at the air,   leaps
and streams like the mane
o a white kelpie-mair.

Spitter, spitter, spitter,
the drip-draps plash,
runklan the quate pool   wrinkling
wi gay mountain gash.   chatter

Pwudle, pwudle,
the deep pool breathes
as oot tae the river
it humphs and heaves.

XI STORMY MUNE

The hump-backit mune crawls through the cloods
like a muckle great horny snail,
ribbonan owre the tenement roofs
a slithery siller trail.
It gars me grue tae feel on my face
the flaff o the wind and the rain's thin lace,
it's that like the sclaff o the cratur's tail.

XII BLAWY NIGHT

Doun on the shore, the lick and lap
o swaws' tongues on glitty stanes;   waves
up in the lift, the scuff and slap
o winds' hauns on the cloods' veins.
They mell in me sae's it's ae soun lingers,
as gin life's pulse was atween my fingers.

XIII   OF SKUNKS AND MEN

The Common Skunk, men call me:
    I do not understand
why for my coat they maul me,
    yet mock my anal gland.

That smelly, yellow evil
    I squirt from bushy tail
is surely no less civil
    than what their tongues exhale?

I stink to gain protection
    from bigger beasts than me;
their words are a projection
    of how they disagree.

While all men are injected
    with lies the other tells,
we skunks are not affected:
    each knows the other smells.

XIV   THE TUNNEL

I wudna gae near thon tunnel gin I was you,
for losh, it's a muckle great dragon's gantan mou!

Frae faur and near, it sooks in screaman trains;
an eftir it's swallow't them hail, you can hear its pains.

It burps out smeik and soot when it's jist had its fill,
but when it gets hungry, it liggs that quate and still.

I wouldna gae near thon dragonish tunnel the nou,
for it's no had a train for hoors, and it micht eat you!

Faint-Hert
(frae the 12th Century Erse)

Douce bell, dulce bell,
   strucken against this wind-blawn nicht,
I'd liefer be keepan tryst wi you   rather
   nor a flichterie woman, faus and licht!

Lily-Lowe

O orange tiger-lily, burnan bricht,
swung lantern at the end o the sun's licht,
your caunel-stamens' drippan yella ase   ash
dazzles the bummers wi its dusty haze;   bees
your silken petals' incandescent flare,
like het, fresh wax, sae mells wi the deep air   mixes
o hinnied Simmer, that I canna tell
jist whaur the blue lift rings the rim o your bell. sky

First Snaw

Sere leaves are crisp, and nae birds caa;
hairst-mists hae smcik't the plums on thc waa;
ilka thing growean trummles at the faa.

Spring wi its green 'll gie youtheid
neist year, and neist, when yirth's nearest deid.
But mair smirran snaw'll be frostan my heid.

On Seeing a Picture o' Johann Christian Fischer in the National Gallery, Edinburgh

Johann Christian Fischer? Mm—the face is kindly,
the wig weil-snod, the features firmly set,
as leanan on a harsichord by Kirkman
wi quill in haun you scrieve a menuet.

The feet sae carefully crossed tae shaw the buckl't shuin,
gimp hose and curly cravat o white lace,
the fiddle on the chair, the music heaped—
the hail, a glisk o 18th Century grace!

Gin ony o your stately airs and tunefu' dances
that kittl't pouther't duchesses lang syne,
culd tinkle oot o Kirkman's yella keyboard,
maist folk 'ud luik at you a second time.

But aa is dusty silence, like the derk ahint you,
and e'en your notes are naethin but a blur;
the background, fu o shaddaws, seems tae draw you
tae hap you in its aa-embracin slur.

Yet there you staun oot still, by Gainsborough made immortal,
as gin sic fame was shairly jist your due—
a perfect shell upon the shore left strandit,
a piece for antiquarians tae view.

J C Fischer (1733-1800) was a German oboeist and composer, born in Freiburg,
who first visited London in 1768 and spent much of his time there. He was friendly
with J C Bach. Fischer married the daughter of Gainsborough, who painted the
portrait that gave rise to this poem.

In the High Street, Edinburgh
(as it wis)

Warriston's Close, Halkerston's Wynd,
crookit and cramped, dim, drauky, blind . . .   damp

High-heapit tenements, lair on lair,
squeezan the licht tae a narra gair;   strip

glaur mair auld nor the stanes themsels   *mud*
gether't in dubs roun court-yaird wells;   *puddles*

doorways and drains that swalla smells,   *swallow*
bluntit as tane wi tither mells;   *one mixed with a*

widdies raxan at wind-flaucht air,   *gallows reaching/wind-blown*
claes wi'oot bodies dancan there;   *clothes*

lawyers hurryan up and doun
frae posher hames in the newer toun;

shoppers aff tae the braw bazaars
o Princes Street in their brun tramcaurs;

kerbside shawlies cryan for sale,
cockels and winkles frae the pail;

auld wives skreichan at shilpit weans,
rickets and history in their banes;

gloaman pubs whaur a frienly stour   *twilight*
shauchles aroun each bricht-lit door;   *shuffles*

the whup-like edge of wir Lallans leid   *whip/tongue*
flick't roun a guilty guideman's heid.

Warriston's Close, Halkerston's Wynd,
where puir folk wantit while judges wined . . .

wemen o pleisure, aulder nor years,
whingean wanchancey worn-oot leers;   *unlucky/looks*

Ramsay, Fergusson, Mary, Knox
thocht less o noo than fear o the pox;

Fegs, and you're gey romantic places   *experience*
for thae wha ainly pree your faces.

Summer Daybreak, Innellan

Drowsily a cock climbs through the first grey
streak that cracks the shapelessness of night;
settles upon a hayrick, claps his wings
and brazenly bugles up another day.
Small creatures furred with darkness slide from sight
as dandily the cock crows, till he springs
the sun from under the hill, aroused to sound
a warmth of waking through the steaming ground.

The sea's the sounding-board for the sun's strings,
tuning the air with trembled chords of light.
Hidden in boughs, unnumbered dew-drenched throats
pour out their diapason of delight
in spraying trills, in tumbling, tendrilled notes,
till every height and fluted hollow sings
the moist new joy of morning, while the sky
makes silence hear and distance magnify.

Early Morning Steamer, Innellan

A wet-nosed morning snuffles around the door,
fawning upon me not to go away;
and I, as if I'd never gone before,
    feel half impelled to stay

as I intercept the sun's awakening scrawl
across the village doused by the browsing hill;
and I hear the stretch of the waves as they yawn and sprawl,
    smiling their aimless fill.

The morning milk-cart jolts its jangling load,
dripping a spitter of stars besides shut gates,
its bored horse pawing sparks from the metalled road
    as he trots, and stops and waits.

The red-cheeked postman's out on his cycled rounds,
ferrying news of beyond through bordered flowers
and, rising from roadside verges, the echoing sounds
    of yesterday's sunny hours.

Don't go, the familiar signals whisper, tempt me;
forget what's to do and succumb to the sense of Now,
where time's unhurried turning breathes Forever,
        only the heart knows how.

Half of me feels these blood-heard urges are right;
that I'll miss one trailing wheel of a Cowal sun,
burning its layer of coloured change by to-night,
        when the news and the milk are done.
Then I think of the way of the world, the buying and selling
that knits it together; how everything's shaped by the mind,
whose insistent inner voice keeps silently calling:
        you daren't get left behind.

The fluttering thump of the fussing paddle-steamer
slows as it sizzles and sidles into the pier.
Hurry, the gangway clatters; *for schemer or dreamer*
        there's no such place as Here.

June Rain

For days the sun had slaked the fields with heat.
Walking the whitened roadway, dusty feet
gritted your breathing's edge. A cricket's beat

scratched on the hayfield stooks its brittle rune.
Not even the spongy shadow of the moon
rubbed out the lazing fever of that June.

And then, one afternoon, came sudden rain.
It slapped and rattled, like a lengthy train
distantly clanking trucks across a plain.

It stroked and soaked each clotted run of earth,
while farmers reckoned up what it was worth,
and politicians claimed they'd staved off dearth.

The scented hedgerows glistened. New light stirred
in trees and bushes. Here and there, a bird
picked up clean notes and tuned them, freshly heard.

Steam Drifter 'Christmas Morn'

Ship from whose hull unfolding nets once shivered
to snare deep miles of water, hung on splinters
of phosphorescent light, your nights lunged brighter
by flash of scales and splash of thudding silver
as, ankle-deep in catch your fishers slithered,
hauling a twitch of ropes keeled full of herring:
the steady-throbbing screw, faint hiss of steam
and oily breath that were your living pulse
are stilled; your broken ribs and gaping deck
swept clean by rains that rake the grey-ribbed sand
where, netted in abandoned rust, you moulder
extinct; a discontinued man-made animal.

Industrial Action

Inside the yard, a hooter shrills;
the cold gates glide open on a height
of frosted girders, rusty-bellied ships
and cranes like one-legged birds, whose metal bills
ask empty questions of the morning light.

Outside, two muffled men twitch lips
counting their cause by heads, and anxiously scan
the cracks in solidarity, how it'll end,
uncertain what the chaffered anger meant
that roared them home one righteous night, and then
slouched their pockets with time not theirs to spend
on buying out the blood's blind discontent.

The Salmon Loup at Gartness

All the collided fusion of spent rain,
twisted and tumbled into braided spills
scouring the rocky channels that constrain
its urgency of falling, heap their chills
of melted distance on the river. Fields,
fringed with coarse meadow-grass and clutching sorrel,
swirl overhangs, till saturation yields
earth, roots and foliage in a cloudy whorl.

Breasting with surge the swollen river rides,
shifting the settled stones that bind its bed,
to gullied boulders steepening its sides
as power like an ocean's roars its head,
plunges the precipice to pound the pool
beneath; a thresh of salmon pink with spawn;
a thumping seethe of spume—the breathless rule
of instinct through cold fishy ages drawn.

Older than words devised to praise or ban,
this call that cries them back to seek the bank,
dankened with shade, where their first days began;
and so they lurk beneath the turgid spank
of clotted froth and dare the slithered rock
that gaps the hammered waters, gathering strength
to launch a height of space; to staunch the shock
of pressure crashing down their scaly length.

Curiously, upon a brittle bridge,
through heatless steam we strain our eyes to stare
at this raw glimpse of nature's tutelage—
for us, a Sunday afternoon's affair;
for them, the desperate thrust and throw of try
and fail. We, sympathising, groan or cheer.
Then suddenly, over the top they fly,
flanks shimmering, a leap that wins them clear
of humanising speculation, deep
to waters where they hang their silver sleep.

Highland Shooting Lodge

Crouched up beneath a crowd of Grampian hills,
this old house waits to hear the report of guns
crisping the Autumn air, for its rooms again
to warm to the jokes of August-trampling men
roughed by the grasp and snap of salmon gills,
the twisted necks of grouse. But nobody comes.

Only, at times, a shapeless horde of cloud
that shifts about the rocky peaks, creeps down
to lick at gutters soured with rotting leaves,
or rub a shapeless back against cold eaves,
then vanish, thin as breath; the drifting shroud
of everything that men once thought they owned.

August in the Highlands

Dampness straddles the moors; a fringing sun
struggles to lift the morning haze through which
men lurk in wait, the ready-loaded gun
angled to aim, ejaculate and pitch
a game-bird's halted flight to heathered earth,
the feathers blooded but the flesh still warm
for soft-mouthed dogs, who know no quarry's worth,
to run for and retrieve from further harm.

Commanding selves, well used to laying sights
on multiple statistics they would own
for general gain, their toasting faces bright
as berries with exertion; yet alone,
and raising only fear; the blundered cry
strained creatures shudder out of earth or sky.

III

Poems from *Snow Warning* (1962),
One Later Day (1964),
This Business of Living (1969)

A View of Loch Lomond

Mountains open their hinged reflections on the loch,
shape and reshape themselves, grow squat or tall,
are bent by shakes of light. We never find
the same place twice; which is why picture postcards
that claim to lay the constant on the table
(the camera cannot lie) are popular;
what trotting tourists hoped to purchase for the shelf;
the image they'd retain, if they were able.

But landscape's an evasion of itself.

Travellers' Tales

The paddle-steamer pulls its own bent image
over loch water, through a rippling screen
that makes itself, tall mountains, trees and islands
            twisted and squat, and seem to lean
out of the shapes of what we think they mean.

Tourists, anonymous behind dark glasses,
admire the scene, yet feel that something's wrong,
they're not sure what; the wind's in the wrong quarter,
            the season's late, the sun's too strong,
the ship's too slow, or perhaps the loch's too long!

According to our childhood expectations
landscape should wear the look of history,
and island waters lap soft, wordless legends.
            No place, wherever it may be,
preserves impersonal objectivity.

Which is why journeys usually disappoint us:
until we're there we always hope to find
escape from discontent, somehow forgetting
            the self we never leave behind
makes all we see half attitude of mind.

Bull Show

Worn men in tweeds from the world's plains and valleys,
women whose breeding's wrapped in rugs and furs,
lounge by the ring where lurching, sweaty herdsmen
with faces that speak seasons, coax and curse
the curly little bulls, taming their paces
to haltered rounds on urine-stenching sand,
far from the trembling fields, the cows of challenge.

Brows marked with thought, marked catalogues in hand,
these well-worn men and well-bred women stare,
seeing, not blackness, curliness nor shape,
nor bull moustaches breathed on frosted air,
but bull that never was; all that a bull should be:
as perfect as their own reality.

Any Night in the Village Pub

Plodding in from the fields of his memory,
he'd shoulder the pub door open, scrape his boots
on the edge of their chatter, order his pint and chaser,
then stand, propped there, a tree pulled up by the roots.

He never argued their odds, nor smirked when they told him
Jock had put Andra's lass in the family way.
When strangers led the talk to the state of the weather,
he'd grunt and glower, as if in his beer the answer lay.

Some said he'd broken his bairnless wife in bedded fury;
that he who mated beasts and seasons, had
no son from his own seed. Others discreetly hinted
living so long alone would drive any man to the bad.

All of them lowered their voices when he joined them,
aware of his self-sufficiency that hung
about the room till he banged down his angry money,
and breenged back into the darkness from which he'd come,
leaving them, oddly disturbed, a whiff of carbolic and dung.

Farm Woman

She left the warmth of her body tucked round her man
before first light, for the byre, where mist and the moist
hot breath of the beasts half-hid the electric veins
of the milking machines. Later, she'd help to hoist
the heavy cans for the tractor to trundle down
to the farm-road end, while her raw hands scoured the dairy.
By seven o'clock, she'd have breakfast on the table,
her kitchen bright as her apron pin, the whole house airy.
Her men-folk out in the fields, the children off to school,
she'd busy herself with the house and the hens. No reasons
clouded the other side of the way she brought
to her man the generous amplitude of the seasons.

Not much of a life, they'd whisper at church soirées
as they watched her chat, her round face buttered with content,
unable to understand that for her each moment
rubbed out the one before, and simply lent
nothing for words of theirs to touch to argument.

Epitaph for a Farmer

Clumsily, like one of his own beasts
made purposeful, he moved through the mud of the steading,
taking no thought of his comfort, mashing his meals,
crumpling an unmade couch, though now and then bedding

some filly girl on the hayrick behind the shed
where the raw cock screeches the mist from each new morning.
Eleven o'clock, and the clatter of his tractor
gave gentle folk in the village shop due warning

to get their business finished, for he'd come in
stramping the cold, his cheek-bones the clouds' bruises,
his clothes steaming of sweat and dung, his strong breath
visible. Not one who gains or loses

at the toss of a season, they said, he racked his joyless days
like generations of his blood before him,
merely to make the earth articulate.
Honour his line; then, if you will, deplore him.

Farm Widow

She moved among the sour smell of her hens' droppings,
her cheeks rubbed to a polish, her skirts bustled
with decent pride; alone since the day the tractor
hauled itself up the field on the hill and toppled

her man away from her. Around her feet
her daughter played, the face of innocence puckered
with the solemn self-importance of being alone
in a grown-up world; her friends, the hens that speckled

her mother's allotment. Some of the weekly folk
who came to buy eggs, watching her counting
their change from the money in her purse, had given her
silent pity, then sensed that she wasn't wanting

anything they could offer; that she seemed
like one whom life had used too soon for writing
some sort of purpose with, her gestures' economies
spelling completeness; gone beyond our waiting

for time and places to happen, behind the will,
to where time and place lie colourless and still.

Kelso Horse Show

Morning discovers it, sprawled in a loop the river
swings itself through the meadow on. Already
horse-boxes, floats and cars have runnelled the edge
of the field to a slush of muddy grass. A steady
straggle of people thickens the booths and the ring.
April neighs coldness. White clouds scud
last winter off the skies. The show-ground shakes
to life as buyers, catalogued with hunches, thud
incautious canters, swerved by the boundary hedge.
Ponies nudge stakes, or rub a child's hand,
soft as their noses. Shouldering knotted halters
the sellers wait their turn behind the stand
where the auctioneer patters, hoarse with loss or profit.

Hunters and hacks parade reluctant paces,
plodding a clomped-up circle. The bidding sways
among five hands, then swings between two faces—
a fighting man whom enemy winds have leathered
smooth as a saddle; and in from the lean hills,
a Border farmer—both of them aware
their urge for satisfaction is the will's
ability to knock down for a song
whatever each has sent his heart upon,
though couldn't care for less as soon as got.
Down goes the Colonel's arrogance; down, down,
before a folly richer than his own.
Hard on the hunter's hooves, a gelding bears
reflections of so many hopeful selves
that most must be unbridled small despairs.
But sold or bought, the time and the place are the horses;
the sweet smell of their sweat, the strung hay
they munch their breath on, the patient stable darkness
rippling their flanks, commotions the livelong day
till it breaks away from its minute-by-minute grazing,
from Countified calls and bawdy Irish curses;
an image riding its own reality
to a sense of recognition no one rehearses;
and for all the human dressage, the play of purses,
something out of the past in me rejoices.

Shetland Pony

A loose fold of steam idling
slumped in a roll of wet grass:
bridle in hand, me, soothing, sidling
up to its rest. One move to pass

the loop round its passivity,
and eyes clench, nostrils itch,
its breath flaring activity
as hocks and neck bend in a twitch

that plucks it up to throw a lunging
proud parabola. It shakes
the field's roots, and leaves me plunging
blundered angles out. It makes

knots in the wide circumference
of centuries it darkly flings
around that less old arrogance
by which my domination clings;

then suddenly trundle-bellies in
from what it's proved to where I stand
haltered in sweat; and, duty done,
nuzzles confinement from my hand.

A Picture of the Caledonian Hunt

Over their fences with superb aplomb
these claret-blooded hunting gentry soar,
their leathering women, mistresshood confirmed
in hourglass stays, with half their years to pour

unquestioned dominance down, curbed in and held
above the silence of their last halloo,
kept from oblivion by the picture's edge
that scuffed their breathless quarry out of view.

Why did they ride to hounds? Some need to assert
the blood's uncertainty, their rulership
of field and ditch? Or, like the pounding fox,
hopeful they'd give their warmest fears the slip?

Or did they straddle stallions to exult
and stretch those instincts men and horses share,
the satisfaction straining thews and sinews
relax into the sense of use and wear?

Did movement threaten from behind scrubbed hedges,
the spring of winter coiled in frosted mould
mock at their privilege, or seem to trap them
nearer the thicket of their growing old?

Still they survive, these lonely, frozen gestures;
the life they leaped at and were ground to, thawed
beneath them, gone with all they thought they stood for.
Yet were they further from whatever flowed

as clarity around their consciousness,
wearing away what living seemed to mean,
but somehow never did, than we are who
catch half-familar glimpses of it, seen

as landscape flowing from a plane is; clean
in its detachment, of itself complete?
What we are left with here are the blanched stains
imprinting lineaments of a defeat

not different from ours, but doubly separated
by the unexplorable geography
of time, each of us on our island of it
misted about in our own difficulty.

Iona: Am bágh cúl na fairge

Basking in the Bay at the Back of the Ocean
lay one black stone the sun could not unglisten;
a smooth wet seal, which neither pulling motion
of wind nor wave could make appear to listen—
night-stillness flapped upon by day's commotion.

Until it suddenly raised its bald old head
and stared at me with the soft eyes of a woman:
gazed in my eyes, as if in them it read
some sign that linked the worlds of seal and human,
then, baffled, flippered silently and fled.

back to its world of aimless seas and tides
holding within blind hands our world, where we
philosophise to straddle the divides
that rob experience of totality,
hinting in such mute glances what it hides.

Hamster

Hamster with the suns of Syria
   doused in your eyes, you stare at me,
   pink fore-feet poised as if you're praying
for some diminutive impossibility.

You climb inside your changeless wheel of wire
   and squeak each treadle-turning spar,
   then curl contented in your nest,
there without having come that far,

and sleep, your purpose for its tiny sake,
   pointlessly rounded and complete.
   Outside, I almost envy you
the satisfaction of your flaying feet.

Aged Four

Alone beside himself, head-in-air
he wanders gently through a fading season,
almost for the last time aware
of how a moment feels, before the lesion

of growing into thought begin to hurt;
the falling burn turn into a complaint
it can't communicate; earth on the hands be dirt
that rubs a sudden scolding up; each feint

the wind boxes the trees with, trace a why
nobody answers; rain be more than wet;
clouds that unfold each other, shape a sky
forecasting portent. Head-in-air, and yet

reluctant to come in, he stands and bawls,
sensing from how much loss his mother calls.

Small Boy Writing

My little son beside me shapes his letters,
a tremulous M, a not-quite-meeting O,
sticking them with his breath down careful pages,
       row on repeated row.

He'll heir the questions elder, self-styled betters
have jumbled from these same laborious signs,
and find what somehow answered for their ages
       has slipped between the lines:

their lingered creeds and dogmas, slackened fetters
no longer strong enough to hold the mind
back from its baffled necessary sieges,
       though nothing's there behind.

He'll find how little we are still their debtors,
their purposes unpurposed, doubts secured
without assurances, their faith's self-pledges,
       loneliness endured.

So may he learn resistance to go-getters
prospecting ends and absolutes; be content
to take delight's quick shapes and sudden edges
       as living's monument.

Picking Apples

Apple time, and the trees brittle with fruit.
My children climb the bent, half-sapping branches
to where the apples, cheeked with the hectic flush
of Autumn, hang. The children bark their haunches

and lean on the edge of their balance. The apples are out
of reach; so they shake the tree. Through a tussle of leaves and
   laughter
the apples thud down; thud on the orchard grasses
in rounded, grave finality, each one after

the other dropping; the muffled sound of them dropping
like suddenly hearing the beats of one's own heart
falling away, as if shaken by some storm
as localised as this. Loading them into the cart,

the sweet smell of their bruises moist in the sun,
their skin's bloom tacky against the touch,
I experience fulfilment, suddenly aware
of some ripe, wordless answer, knowing no such

answers exist; only questions, questions, the beating years,
the dropped apples . . . the kind of touch and go
that poetry makes satisfaction of;
reality, with nothing more to show

than a brush of branches, time and the apples falling,
and shrill among the leaves, children impatiently calling.

Royal Visit

Several hours before the ceremonial
scuffed schoolchildren shuffle into the Square,
clutching imported flags for semaphoring
excitement at being out and otherwhere.

The stately car of celebration, gliding
down rows of cheering, rolls its public way,
with everyone the better for its passing
although quite why they couldn't really say.

Cheer upon waving cheer trails on, receding
to private distance. The lining of the Square
collapses. *Wasn't she lovely?*, the grown-ups gooed
while the children munch and, chattering, get shooed
back to their class; too young to be aware
why the real big moment happened before it had been,
and had little to do with a vaguely smiling Queen.

School Prizegiving

The voice rose out of his enormous paunch
reverberant with wisdom rounded there
since he had stood, a sliver of himself,
with boys like these in some lost otherwhere

innumerable platitudes away.
And yet, for all its width, the voice was small,
smooth-feathered still, cock-crested in success
that time had caponed, centre of the hall.

And as his little meanings strutted out
in preening words, the eager fledgling boys
who listened must have wondered if they too
might one day make the same wing-beating noise.

to keep their courage up, their run of years
inexplicably fouled, their hopeful hastes
turned back upon themselves; each still so sure
he'd force his way beyond these middle wastes . . .

And I, aware how satisfaction breaks
against its realisation, and how thick
the darkness gathers, caught myself, ashamed,
half-murmuring: *Their prizes, masters, quick!*

Harbour Inn

Propped up against the bar, his old face wrinkled
with salty oaths, he'd run the dialogue
of wind and waves for anyone who'd listen,
to compass him against the gathering fog.
Most of his tales blew truer for the telling;
yet between doomed ships nursed out from under
a fold of storms, and girls he'd briefly handled
in ports whose names spelled unaccustomed wonder,
lonely upon some deck of dignity
he'd rise from nowhere, wet each livelong day
up to its eyes, and spit upon what carries
the yielded flesh of ships and girls away.

At Hans Christian Andersen's Birthplace, Odense, Denmark

Sunlight folds back pages of quiet shadows
against the whitewashed walls of his birthplace. Tourists move
through crowded antiseptic rooms and ponder
what row after row of glass-cased papers ought to prove.

Somehow the long-nosed gangling boy who was only
at home in fairyland, has left no clues.
The tinder-box of Time we rub
answers us each the way we choose.

For kings have now no daughters left for prizes.
Swineherds must remain swineherds; and no spell
can make the good man prince; psychiatrists
have dredged up wonder from the wishing well.

The whole of his terrible, tiny world might be
dismissed as a beautiful madman's dream, but that each of us knows
whenever we move out from the warmth of our loneliness
we may be wearing the Emperor's new clothes.

Mozart's Salzburg

Age after age this rock that reared a castle
where Prince-Archbishops staved time and its wars at bay,
grew stately halls on stems of corridors
that now drain back their legends. Day after day

guides patter up the ghosts of pleasured men
whom splendour dignified with destiny; turned cold,
their comfortless pomp now clothed in fountained stone:
men without pietas, most of them utterly loathed.

We are shephereded to where the past stopped
for this place. Napoleon broke the spell
of gracious iron blessing: the last Archbishop
gathered his robes and fled, the guides tell

us in several languages. Yet who would care
what made one tyranny different from another
if a man with staring eyes and backstair jokes
hadn't served up music that small-talk couldn't smother;

a fellow too big for his boots who didn't seem worth his pay,
sounding his age to agelessness, beyond the reach of their say.

In Shetland

I   ON THE QUAY

Gulls brake hard on their cries,
scatter droppings round the backs
of fishermen sliding scuffed boxes
wet with a darling catch of cran.

Here and there a headless herring,
dawn-bled by the nets, tempts
gulls to drop the white pulse
of distance they morosely keep
up over the roofless castle.

Weather-toughened scraps for crofters,
salted winters or good years
once in the castle's blackened cellars,
there's been hunger's picking-edge
here since land first broke waters.

Visitors, cork-floats and nets
colour up the tarry quay,
till night douses gulls and castle,
boats rib the wound open
and the sea's blood keel-hauls
the like event that is this place.

II SUDDEN STORM

Slaps of light flare, like bits
of dropped sky, commotioned brown
by the spring turf they land on,
each and all a heather-eye
cocked against the lifted squalls
cliffs can't shrug back to sea.

Here and there a burn runs
away with itself, no river
lazing loops to wind it in.
Here and there a heron hoists
unsteady stalks and launches up,
a lump of flung earth flying.

Haystacks roped with hung stones,
crofts that no gale's untied,
coorie down on green strips
swathed out of sour seasons;
peat blots the rain, scouring
winds dunt against each other.

Girls in boxed beds fear
the storm's litany of rage
mouthed against the croft's shoulders,
while the sea sucks and snatches
what their men clutch; a living
from the sparse edge of distance.

Early Morning Fisher

Stubbed at the pond's edge, blunted by his pipe,
his eyes are lined to the rod he strings and flails
through delicate arcs that flick the air with water.
Posing its own question a swan sails
over its answers. Unconcerned, its mate
glides out from the rushes, shaping the breeze
that shifts the thin mist blenched from the back of darkness
to kindle dawn among the smoking trees.

Day broadens. The fisherman spreads his patience
angled only to tense and trap the bite
slashing the pond's translucence, sliver-knife
that flashes cold through cunning out of sight,
the pulse in that green-bottled ooze of light
each morning lairs afresh with a rocking light.

At the Mouth of the Ardyne

The water rubs against itself,
glancing many faces at me.
One winces as the dropped fly
tears its tension. Then it heals.

Being torn doesn't matter.
The water just goes on saying
all that water has to say,
what the dead come back to.

Then a scar opens.
Something of water is ripped out,
a struggle with swung air.
I batter it on a loaf of stone.

The water turns passing faces,
innumerable pieces of silver.
I wash my hands, pack up, and
go home wishing I hadn't come.

Later, I eat my guilt.

Stones in Sky and Water

Under the lap of water sunken stones change
their indefinable shapes. A dazzle gleams
from the roof-tops of ripples. Summer's bright-
ness peoples the loch with moveless stir that seems
to mingle height and distance. Clouds free-range,
trailing their aimless shadows. Water's peace
gets rubbed against by winds that peel off light.
But the smooth-bending forms the stones release
float upwards like cast images, to exchange
the appearance for reality and spring
fresh impulses, the flux of all delight
a moment in eternity can bring
when stones in sky and water silently sing.

Solway Fisherman

He rubs shoulders awkwardly in shops,
as if landed by one of his own nets
where tins and reaching arms and used-up breath
and jostled noise accumulate like debts

through which the likes of him can scarcely move,
for all the heavy slowness of his speech,
the weight of silence in his eyes; as if
he'd only be at ease when he could breach

again what holds this town together,
pilot his pipe between the sanded bars
that shift about the harbour, and sit free
to stare his empty thoughts at clouds and stars.

Night veering that rubbed shade on his jowl;
the fret of mist, winds' auguries and the sea,
run him so high his blood's their element;
the dark side of our numerous jollity.

This Business of Living

Midges fasten their mist-cloud over the river,
zizzing and zazzing, stitching intricacy,
an uncolliding shimmer, a pattern
that satisfies some midge necessity.

A wind, shuttling through roots of weeds and grasses,
side-slips against the weave of their symmetry
and breaks its shape. The rupture shifts, is mended,
then suddenly struck by a thrust of energy,

the water twists up out of its element;
a kick of trout that heels midges from air,
recoiling under its own ripples, leaving
torn suspension, a gapped bite to repair.

Immediately the chromosomes reshuffle
to push the mist-cloud back to its old form,
and I, on the bank, experience satisfaction,
watching a small completeness assert its norm.

Love's Anniversaries
(for Joyce)

It was the generosity of delight
that first we learned in a sparsely-furnished flat
clothed in our lovers' nakedness. By night
we timidly entered what we marvelled at,

ranging the flesh's compass. But by day
we fell together, fierce with awkwardness
that window-light and scattered clothing lay
impassive round such urgent happiness.

Now, children, years and many rooms away,
and tired with experience, we climb the stairs
to our well-furnished room; undress, and say
familiar words for love; and from the cares

that back us, turn together and once more seek
the warmth of wonder each to the other meant
so strong ago, and with known bodies speak
the unutterable language of content.

These Two Lovers

At any moment of the day
you'll suddenly turn to me and say:
'Tell me you love me.' So I do.
Yet, as I pass the words to you,
sometimes, preoccupied, my nuance
seems to deny you the assurance
you need so urgently. And I
find myself challenged to deny
the opposite of what I mean.
A sightless distance blurts between
us two, and I then re-discover
how islanded is loved from lover.

When all pretensions are unmade
and we together lie in bed
as lovers do, our bodies' act
renews the temporary pact
that shores a little warming grace
from the cold wash of nothingness.
But though you curl into my side,
fulfilled and sleepy, the divide
that mists us all swirls back, and I
watch the Plough rust against the sky,
the sense of person and of place
sieved through the fall-away of space.

Until, unconsciously, you press
my hand against your nakedness.
Pulling me back to now and here,
you narrow distance from my fear.
I feel your breathing, and am sure
however torn or insecure
the lineaments of human trust,
our bodies' simple touching lust
tautens a wholeness running through
the variants of me and you,
so turn to sleep; like you, content
should this togetherness we're lent
prove to be all that living meant.

A Ballad of Orpheus

On the third day after her unexpected death,
Orpheus descended into Hell.
It wasn't hard to find. He knew the directions well;
asleep, he'd often read them by the light of his own breath.

The doorkeeper was surly, but let him in;
he had no reason to keep anyone out.
Glaring like a lit city, a kind of visible shout
fungused about the place, an absolute din

of all notes, overtones and unheard sounds at once.
To keep his sense of self intact, he struck
a few familiar chords, and as his luck
would have it, she, who all along had felt a hunch

something unusual would happen, heard the order
and limiting purpose of his playing; and being not yet
fully subtracted out of herself to fit
Hell's edgeless ambiguities, broke from the border

of blurring dissolution, and moved towards her lover
as a cloud might move in the world of gods above.
He guessed that shape and stir to be his love
Eurydice, well knowing that no other

idea of woman would answer to the lyre
that sang against his loins. She came to him crying
aloud her numbed womanly tenderness, trying
to warm her cold half-body at the core of his fire.

But without a word said, he seized her hand
and began pulling her roughly along the road,
past the doorkeeper, who smirked, seeing the load
he carried. She, being woman, couldn't understand

that love in action needs no drag of speech,
and pled with him to turn round once and kiss
her. Of all the conditions the gods had imposed, this
was the one he dared not disobey. Reproach

followed reproach; till, as he fled
through shadow to shadow, suddenly it seemed
that the only absolute good was what he'd dreamed
of her. So Orpheus stopped, and slowly turned his head.

At once she began to small. He watched her disappear
backwards from him, and thought it best
that things should be so. How could he have stood the test
of constant loving, always with the fear

of his first loss ahead of him again,
believing happiness ends in boredom or pain?
So Orpheus returned by the same lane
as he went down by, to compose himself in a world of men.

A Picture by Anne Redpath

A pure white porcelain arrangement of
peonies, mid-wintered snow on snow
cooling the scented blush and flush of summer
that curls about it; flow within a flow
which somehow to the seeing eye suggests
a balancing perfection; fabled bliss
of angels singing silence they suspend from,
open as light that pours out praise. Yet this
moment, no longer moment but a rubbed-
off edge of mind on movement, the bright quick
of passing disconnected from its distance—
holds nowhere we could lose ourselves in, stuck
each thickly in our separate difficulties.
A pure arrangement of bestowed repose
leaves us amid the imperfect flux, defining
what order the imagination shows.

Where and Now

Thick in the pluck of bramble-getting,
a big-toothed nettle bites my hands.
The stinging of its saw-mark whitens,
and a lost slip of boyhood stands
in sixteen years of tares and tangle,
whey-faced against the world's advance,
brushed-at by gobs of cuckoo-spit,
spilt like his own lost innocence.
With easy-milking thoughts he laced
bitter and sweet, cow-parsley curds,
and kissed the honey-suckle girls
who crossed their golden sex with words.

Stained fingers on the bruise of fruit
probing so blindly they should touch
that sapped prolificacy, stretched
across the rank-blood nettle's reach,
and pluck a ghost who could not come
from that lost *Where* he grew among;
whose thoughtful substance now is dumb!

May Day Demonstration

Chunky together, the marchers blacken their way
through the blanched Sunday streets to the public park
where banners thump the air, bands play
against each other, and children shout and lark

around the moving feet of solemnity.
In drip-dried letters, six men grimly bear
above the crowd the moment's ragged complaint;
which is largely irrelevant. For what the speakers share.

from their platform is the wordless rage
of us all against the chance, the change and the dark;
subscribers to the human document
who have nothing to sign it with but a blunt mark.

Accident Report

A man with a crumpled chest, a woman gone with child,
and a boy of five, neck broken, scarcely breathing,
cool in their own blood. From a flurry of bells
two men leap down and begin efficiently heaving

the stretchered bodies into the ambulance,
and box its doors on the worst of the whole affair.
It rocks and sways through blue and white alarm
three people past all hope of human repair

to the hospital it makes its sallies from.
Meanwhile a policeman blots their blood with sawdust;
another stoops to measure suddenness,
as if from twenty screaming yards the law must

somehow exact an answer that restores
normality. Two cars, crouched in the shape
of fixed obscenities, drain like burst animals.
Edging cautiously part, the rest of us gape.

are fascinated; smell the moment of strike
that—Christ!—how narrowly missed us, yet happened far
enough away to blame on luck or carelessness,
and exorcise the raw decline we are.

Market Values

Dressed in the shabbiest of pleasantries,
he'd joked through five and thirty years of selling
The Product. Best of its kind—the makers said so.
The price, of course, had frothed up from the shilling

it cost when first he'd seeped his mind in Soapsy,
the Suddsiest Suds, and swallowed the Company line,
not noticing the hidden hook and sinker
beneath the lather, 'fresh as moorland pine,'

that dried him out among the shimmering clichés—
'Far more soap for much less than your money';
'Cleaner than clean,' so one ahead of God—
the temporary job that by some funny

mischance of luck turned out to be for keeps.
At first his wages fed him the illusion
he'd weekend freedom with the kids and wife,
a pension to grow old for. Such confusion

as gritted his uneasy self-assurance,
he rinsed out on his customers. 'The view
the Company takes is a generous one, and so,
quite naturally, they're anxious not to sue.'

(Less generous, by Christ, to me than you!)
But gradually, the texture of the fabric
he thought of as his soul wore limp and thin,
and wouldn't stiffen to the starchy rubric.

of sales-promotion hand-outs. The Directors,
whose futures followed underlying trends,
said he'd outlived his usefulness. They sacked him,
those faceless ones who look like dividends,
ten years before he'd run the final paces
to pass the winning-post for burnt-out cases.

Failure

The uncertainty he slinks with into the pub
where frothy men are bandying loud content
across the bare-worn counter, is his only
certainty. Its nagging doesn't relent,

a thin, gut-scraping shadow, lacerating
the lining of his small-talk, overlaying
his nakedness of love; the only question
he's never found the proper words for saying.

So he drinks until his speech leaks at the seams—
who knows, an answer might seep through that way
and shake his sober doubtings to their senses
there, in the clear light of the others' day?—

drinks till he frees the chaffering misery
of chasing what he knows he'll never find
and couldn't face now; drinks to ensure he's fuddled
a too-late answer forming in his mind.

Poor Jock, they say. A bloody good war record.
Five Jerries single-handed. There's his wife,
of course, that trouble with the business.
It's queer the run that some folk get from life.

Café Politician

Shaken blousily loose by the clatter of trays,
swing-doors bumping her bottom, armpits breathing
as she leans across the table, swiping at crumbs,
pocketing small change under saucer and cup,
she rattles down warm cutlery and says
her ducks-and-dearies what'll-you-have, though seething
with weariness; as if nothing ever comes
between next fetch-and-carry and last wash-up.

What might have happened to her once, who cares
to think about? Surely she must have been pretty
enough not just to be left alone to wait
while battered kitchen swing-doors flipped away
her youth? The patient to-and-froing she wears
earned her more than a pittance tipped with pity?

Sir, don't sit dreaming over that empty plate;
we want to get finished; you're causing us delay;
it's a dull Jill that's all work and no play.

Glasgow Nocturne

Materialised from the flaked stones of buildings
dank with neglect and poverty, the pack,
thick-shouldered, slunk through rows of offices
squirting anonymous walls with their own lack

of self-identity. *Tongs ya bass, Fleet,*
Fuck the Pope spurted like blood; a smear
protesting to the passing daylight folk
the prowled-up edge of menace, the spoor of fear

that many waters cannot quench, or wash
clean from what hands, what eyes, from what hurt hearts?
O Lord! the preacher posed at the park gates,
what must we do to be whole in all our parts?

Late on Saturday night, when shop fronts doused
their furniture, contraceptives, clothes and shoes,
violence sneaked out in banded courage,
bored with hopelessness that has nothing to lose.

A side-street shadow eyed two lovers together;
he, lured from the loyalties of the gang
by a waif who wore her sex like a cheap trinket;
she, touched to her woman's need by his strong

tenderness. On the way from their first dance,
the taste of not enough fumbled their search
of hands and lips endeared in a derelict close.
Over the flarepath of their love, a lurch

thrust from the shadow, circling their twined bodies.
It left them clung before its narrowing threat
till she shrieked. They peeled her from her lover,
a crumpled sob of a doll dropped in the street,

while he received his lesson; ribs and jaw
broken, kidneys and testicle ruptured, a slit
where the knife licked his groin. Before he died
in the ambulance, she'd vanished. Shops lit

up their furniture, contraceptives, clothes and shoes
again. Next morning, there was a darker stain
than *Tongs ya bass* and *Fleet* on the edge of the kerb;
but it disappeared in the afternoon rain.

Attending a Football Match

It sneaked past watchful attendants,
warned to be on the look-out for It
among the male together-noise.
White faces on dark clothes
cohered, shading the terracing
to the anonymous crouch of a crowd.

The ninepin players trotted in.
Kinetic muscles moved in play,
and Matt, John, Jock and Wullie
bounced on their excitement's cheers.

But as the ball began to score
goals spent in a stretched net,
It wedged Itself between the roars
of the single-backed, two-minded thing,
for *game*, insinuated *name*,
a syllableless, faceless feeling
of nothing words identified.

Then suddenly It broke loose—
bottles hit fists and screams.
Police tore the crowd apart
to get It. It eluded them.

From spectators crushed by shock,
a swearing vanful of louts,
the cut-up quiet in hospitals,
no real evidence could be taken.
Charges were, of course, preferred—
disorderly conduct, obstructing the police—
but no one found out what It was,
or whose It is, or where It came from.

Seen Out

Over small print in papers,
arguments at Public Inquiries,
a demolition squad moves in;
coloured helmets swarming up to
patched roofs, unpicking rafters,
levering slabs through ceilings,
gulping cupboards sheer with air.

Now and then a tenement
fights back, stumps snarling
chokes of dust, menacing
what once had been a passing street.
Machines bring all stone
down to its own level.

On a half-cleared site where soon
rows of red and yellow curtains
would be switched-on stacks of light,
I found the handle of a pan,
a mattress spring, a chair's leg,
the bric-a-brac of done-with caring;
while from one grey isolated
tenement storey, with cushions,
blandishments and blankets
they prised loose an old woman
from a sense of place that hadn't
quite seen out her time.

Requiem for a Burgh Cleaner

Bumphled with years beneath a shabby coat,
he looked as if the Burgh winds had clotted
him blue with cold that stiffened every movement
behind the brush-and-cart he pushed at rotted
strands of wizened summers, dead and gone;
papers stripped of the urgency they'd guarded,
the hopes and fears of yesterday discarded.

They've swept him to the cemetery, where leaves
moulder the earth and paper sogs to mush,
while lorries slouch around his avenues;
devouring jaws that chomp the detritus
which refuse operators toss to them;
a life-style ready-ripped from handy packs,
its monument, wet piles of plastic sacks.

Last Post

A postcard posted in the reign of King Edward VII has just been delivered to the address for which it was intended. The present occupant of the house has no knowledge of the person to whom it was addressed. A Post Office spokesman said they had no idea why it had taken so long to reach its destination.   Radio News Item

Long skirts sweeping sepia pavements, hats
like birds nestling on startled human faces,
cars creaked to their spokey wheels, small chat
caught in a crack of sixty years ago
fluttering free to our unstructured present:
an age that knew its places and its betters
face upwards with my morning's bills and letters.

The seaside villas haven't changed their posture
since that Edwardian summer, when the weather
was 'simply grand', X marked the bedroom window
of 'Loving Liz,' the question *when or whether?*
got breathed into her postscript, 'wish you were here,'
Xs criss-crossing 'oh, my dear, my dear!'

Dear Liz, I can't reply, but hope the longing,
stretched by the week that grew your absence fonder,
lasted the lust of wars, the years of wronging
that lie between my present and your yonder;
that you embraced a warmth of flesh's needing
from him who should have read what I'm now reading;

that ruling age, when scoring off your beauty
on children, the short length of love's content,
allowed you beg the question of its ending,
acceptance being all that age is lent,
since neither pleading prayers nor praises sound
across death's nothingness, where no one's found.

Speaking of Scotland

What do you mean when you speak of Scotland?
The grey defeats that are dead and gone
behind the legends each generation
savours afresh, yet can't live on?

Lowland farms with their broad acres
peopling crops? The colder earth
of the North East? Or Highland mountains
shouldering up their rocky dearth?

Inheritance of guilt that our country
has never stood where we feel she should?
A nagging threat of unfinished struggle
somehow forever lost in the blood?

Scotland's a sense of change, an endless
becoming for which there was never a kind
of wholeness or ultimate category.
Scotland's an attitude of mind.

IV

Poems from *Comings and Going* (1971),
Selected Poems 1942–72 (1973),
The Run from Life (1975)

Girl Reading a Letter

Clutching unopened a newly-delivered letter,
girl, sitting beside me in the bus,
full of too much, the flare of your breasts and the flush
of your crossed legs the lack of some man's delight;
how the ripe roundness, the soft unplucked promise
shrinks as your eyes pick withering from its pages,
and your body's stalked, as if for the first time,
by the gravity that pulls us all to the ground.

Games Mistress

Always, and for its own sake, the game!
There was no other way for hopeful girls
to win their colours in the trials ahead
(necessarily unspecified beyond the
boundaries of school hymn and hockey pitch).
Generations careering towards this goal
coached from the side by her antiseptic figure,
upright as chastity, forwarding the game
that left her changeless on the cheering line.

    Breath's taste in the kiss
    against a hard-pressed door;
    the steamed-up hand in the car
    loosening motor senses;
    the public bromide wedding
    and honied harvestmoon;
    legs arched for the trawl
    of children out of birth;
    the scarcely-noticed growth of
    affection stronger than limbs;
    cancer's surprise;
    an ageing belly heaving
    from dried-out opposite—

Fifty years backwards, through astonished tears,
some old girls gave her a silver hockey stick
with names of distinguished pupils carved upon it.
To this, of course, no game could be attached.

The Vacant Chair

Suddenly, they broke out
of the discipline of absorbing facts
as if there really were such things.
Suddenly, they wanted to ask,
and have answered, the awkward questions.

Why scientists calculated
the cheapest form of total explosion?
Why children's bellies distended
with the needless obscenity of hunger?
Priests be permitted to father poverty
under the bedclothes of superstition?
Why those whom age had cataracted
with inoperable complacency
should profess to teach each generation
as if such blindness didn't exist?

A reasonable line was taken
by public and Press for a little while.
But at last they whom the blindness most
affected began to get angry. Who
were the young to expect answers for questions,
actions for needs? Why couldn't they stay
closed in their studies, leaving life
to settle at its own level,
accepting the absence of solutions?
After all, what they wanted
was, clearly, a Chair of Impossibilities.

And who could they have found to fill it?

Two Generations

A twig cracked, no louder than
a bone snapped in a furred trap.
Rabbits can't size fear. One flopped
across our harmless track slap

into the blue bolt a stoat
launched from a farm gate.
Fangs fastened the neck's shriek,
a cold killing without hate.

Stop it, the child cried: *Oh, why don't you stop it?*
face to face with what has no stop,
and the useless pity that brought down
the back of my hand in a sharp chop.

Feeling Small

The coldest day for thirty years.

Scuffed among the stained snow
of petrol pumps, a thrush hung out
its broken wing, the grounded eyes
glazed with a finishing of fear.
Before long, I thought, a car
will crunch it quickly, or someone else
snap its neck against a stone.
I turned away, reproaching myself
for wasting pity on a small bird,
so much that's larger claiming pity.

It had gone when I got back,
cleanly, without blood or feathers.
I was able to drive home
to dinner, television news
from which all essences of pity
had been most carefully extracted;
make good my warm accustomed loves.

The coldest day for thirty years.

Certain Killers

You'd think a mouse so mere a thing
it shouldn't be too hard to kill.

Men believe it crumbs germs
from daily swept-under boards;
women shriek up chairs for fear
it runs against their privacies.

I laid a baited trap. By night
the sprung bar pushed eyes
out of the crushed head. By day
blood ran down disposable whiskers.

I could, of course, keep a cat
to eat my scraps of chopped meat;
but I like birds—they keep their distance—
and cats think all cheeps
signal their pounce of destruction.
Besides, I don't think I could stand
being contempt's glared target
for not doing my own small murders.

Nameless

You step from underthings,
lie down beside me.
What we touch is earth
parched with explanation.

Rain over Eden
feels its way across us.

Trembling, it spills
unexplained release.

Fruits

She rolled the Easter egg of her belly
through the pinging-open door
to lean her turn against the earth
smell of vegetables. As he rang
the till on chatter of last night's telly,
he noticed stains like sour sapples,
detergent hands, bare legs veined
blue by seven kids in as many
years. Eve with all her Eden drained,
she shook out her last penny.
He handed her back bruised apples.

Shore Leave, Amsterdam

Perched in a window, fish-net sex for sale,
she lured her baited breasts with naked smiles
to hook attention. *Like to come in?*, eyes asked.
Price fixed, he stumbled through a shabby door
into an over-heated room, and took off
embarrassed trousers. *You must wear this*, she said;
*to keep me clean. Only the Spanish gentlemen
won't, because of their religion. Ah! a good one
you have there. Together we'll have fun.
Help me undress.* The cleeks of her taut bodice
thickened beneath the flustered pluck of his fingers. . . .

Straddling his loins, she rode his fantasy
back to where it had risen from; dismounted,
and left him lying, limply disappointed,
to dress awkwardly, pass the time of day.

                         . . . Are you a local girl?
The season good for tourists? Had fine weather?

Schoolmarm comforting little boy, she patted
him on the head of his conversational strain,
shook hands, re-locked her apartment door, and left him
beside the rain-pocked slough of a canal.

Anon

They are excavating the mound at the foot of the village,
young men with gentle eyes and curious beards,
and names like Brown and Soutar, and soft-breasted girls
on whom they'll one day stamp their borrowed image,
name upon name. What else have they to preserve?

They are digging for signs. How like were the other Browns
and Soutars, ripening out of the blameless soil,
and having to leave their names when it took them under?
Turning over the freshly wounded earth,
only Anon stares out from whitened bone.

A Change of Fashion

On Summer holidays
my trouser turn-ups collected grains of sand,
pieces of shells and other memorabilia.

On earning days
I'd brush out these dried sights of sea and sky
to make way for the hairs of casual carpets.

You can't gather
capsuled space in trousers;
so now we've done away with turn-ups, and are
becoming less familiar with ourselves.

One Day at Shieldaig

Behind rolled Vauxhall windows
two women, sealed in homely Aran sweaters,
knitted their fingers into sweated Arans.

Two men cast off for
'a breath of air' (discreetly to water themselves),
came sweating back, two strolling Arans homing.

Even the clouds and mountains
got knitted up in patterns of each other,
the sea's fingers glinting incredibly.

Christmas Cards

I *THREE KINGS TALKING*

After it was over, together in the sun,
three specialists in ruling, they compared
   notes, as farmers or carpenters might
warm to each other over the craft they shared.

One said: Although, of course, I'm no
believer in old wives' tales or popular rhymes,
   we have to take new situations
within the accepted context of the times.

For most, the times are never good,
as you both know. The idea of a saviour
   come as a babe caught people's fancy.
There seemed little chance of riotous behaviour

over one so young, as long
as I fell in with their much-talked-of whim
   that what I had to do was follow
that strange, fast-moving star to come upon him.

The second said: Though it got you here,
we're all of us men of the world, and well aware
   that in the present state of knowledge
one can't account for what makes the simple stare.

The fact is, in my kingdom there was
unrest, dissatisfaction with the ruling line.
   Nothing you could single out;
unrest, a communal waiting for some sign

that the heat and the flies and the shortage of food
they had to put up with—the sheer injustice of
   their lot—wasn't all that life
had to offer. I certainly don't mean to scoff

at the kind of let-out this promised saviour
brings. If the gold, the frankincense and myrrh
   we've proffered in that stable buys us
relief from trouble, quells any possible stir

a minority of dissidents might
have fanned up into open revolution,
    our journeys will have been worth while.
A child can't overthrow a constitution.

The third said: No doubt you're both right,
I don't think I'll forget that mother's face.
    A strange thing, too, the three of us
should come from the earth's ends to this untidy place

we'd none of us heard of. Whatever the why
or the wherefore, we've done the sensible thing.
    If the child is holy, he'll be talked of
for longer than any politician or king.

Let us keep silence over the reasons
each of us used to get here, and then go
    our ways, do what needs to be doing,
say what's expected of us, and who's to know

of our understandable difficulties?
These three kings parted, each with his own rich train
    of satisfied diplomacy.
What happened next? They were never heard of again.

II A KNOCK AT THE DOOR

Three merchants paused over their wine—
a strange hubbub so late at night,
the innkeeper on a strong line,
the raised voices out of sight.

Could they be Romans, come to take
for questioning some wretch whose fear
the country's peace made think might shake
off guilty scent? A quick peer

behind closed curtains, and one said:
An old man with skirt-lifting stuff
came here to litter. There's no bed.
I got the last. Straw's good enough

for them. Not guessing that the child
waiting to breach the puzzled womb
imagined angels had assailed,
would need a legend's length for room.

III   CHRISTMAS EVE

Plastic lights and wrapping paper; preparations
for giving, getting and eating; all are done.
We've paid once more the annual reparation
most of us don't believe in: a virgin's son

come to forgive flesh, pronouncing purpose
over confusion, the garbage of history—
not what the public faces so blandly rehearse,
but the nameless ones for whom boredom's the mystery

only a tribalistic myth makes bearable,
with its everlasting promise of recompense.
For the time being, neuroses are shareable,
profitless kindness yields some sort of sense,

hinted accord, an immanence unstilled
from whatever plangent meaning earth can show.
When such cold comfort carols me, I'm lulled
to thankfulness that wonder doesn't let go.

IV   ON THE MANTELPIECE

Once more the old mythologies reassemble—
reindeer and angels canopy the city street
with *lux aeterna* while the clausing crowd's
cash-registered and carolled at supermarket heat.

Firs in tenement windows signature
in glittering cones of light the birth that needs no bed,
our public three-weeks' drying out of conscience
needling unhoovered carpets with their country spread.

Sceptics or sinners, none of us wise men,
for the most part aware that there's no beckoning star
to guide our possibilities, reflect
once more on where and what and why we think we are.

In this brief glow that warms our winter solstice
out of its ancient future-holding cold, our blood
reaches us towards its kind, and in rejoicing
preaches an incomplete and temporary good,
the raised glass pressure of our festive mood,
all that we know of it, or ever could.

Travelling Folk

Cornered in wastes of land, spinnies of old roads
lopped back from the new, where done horses
leant once on starved haunches, battered cars
nuzzle scrunted bushes and caravans.

Copper-breasted women suckle defiance
at schools inspectors. Sanitary men
are met with bronze-age scowls. All to no purpose.
Blown across Europe's centuries, bound only

in piths and withies to settlements not moved
by permanent impermanencies—smokey
violins, dusks gathered from skies
purple as hedge-fruits, or plucked stolen chickens—

these exiles from our human order seed
in the rough, overlooked verges of living,
their stubborn litter filling with vagrancy,
the cracks our need for conformation shows.

Dunvegan: The Great Music

Three centuries of shadow fallen
from boastful, proud or threatened chiefs,
a honed edge of music moving
more than was MacLeod's to command.
Eight notes to snurl a galley buffeting
the Minch of battle; cover a bride
with bloodied history, begetting
more than flesh's green delight;
mindlessly march men to meet
vengeance narrowed to a glen,
or rally distance to strange causes
on foreign fields where poppies grow;
set simple feet dancing
bare measures of unconcern;
intricately mourn whole generations
gone down to treachery or storm.

Slabs in a roofless church relate
chiefs to the remnant of stone legend.
Knowing their place, the MacCrimmons wait
outside, where Hebridean winds
chanter their stopped, sodden ears
with whistling tunes of glory, grass
scythed by silent tongues of nettles.

A Mass of Mozart's

Rococo angels chub their puffy cheeks;
filigree sunshine filters cream and gold
through sainted windows; consolation gleams,
unquestionable as authority;
a sensuous arras hangs, and flames of candles
lean to it, breathing out their soft hosannas.

Agnus dei, who took away the sins
of the eighteenth-century world where Mozart poured
his order and assurance through these words
worn smooth by Latin centuries, for me,
Kyrie eleison, sceptic shadows lie
along the mind's cold crevices. The chill of faithful
stone that has outlived its common purpose
no longer shields to bless. Yet the unanswerable

Dona nobis pacem soars above
these gilded prayers, those rafters of belief;
and though no heaven holds the judgment winds'
four corners, and the old imagined earth
turns aimless, there's at least the heart's Amen
that music moulds such certain transiencies.

Overture Leonora Number Next

In a sense there was nothing left but anti-climax
when at last the surging heroics had to stop
with Freedom, noble and serene in triumph,
applauded past the final curtain-drop.

But the Minister had to take his anonymity
back to its office; see that there was got
in train the customary procedures
for having political prisoners discreetly shot;

Fidelio strip off her male disguises,
take on her Florestan's love and come to bear
and rear his children, the common lot of women
whatever clothes or circumstance they wear.

The prisoners found they'd lost the art of singing
rapt choruses to the age-old ultimate foe
all peasants have to reckon with, deaf poverty,
leaving them life, but little else to show.

What of those weedy soldiers who'd obeyed
Pizarro's orders, whose defeat they'd cheered?
They betted on how long they'd lounge in barracks
before the same old sequence reappeared.

Responsibilities

They stand in line, stiff as their own rifles,
guards of honour glanced at by Heads of State;
frozen opera choruses who, at a moment's notice
transform themselves to an instrument of hate.

Professional killers trained in the latest methods
of ending lives regardless of sex or age,
destroying whatever civilisation's brought together
without questioning why or what they engage.

Faceless opponents sheltered by safer distance,
unquotable by historians, their names
listed to be forgotten on memorials;
means to their own end, but others' aims.

Children are taught this leader or that king
built castles and scored victories; his battle scars,
honour and guilt inextricably mixed.
Who laid the stones, put death into his wars?

Subjective Projective

amber
slow up
red red—

clicky clack clack domenico scarlatti
open the window
breathe fresh pollution
quite a belly that girl's carrying
wonder if she got it in bed
or in the back of some man's car
defending women's right to freedom
whatever the christ that is—

did he spit down that drain
just because the drain was there
gaping up at him
god
the permissive society—

hairy enough to be a poet
too damn many of them
any bugger can be a poet
now that you can't nail thoughts with rhyme
or even have thoughts
too old fashioned for collapsing society
the sunday critics cry
wishing they could write poems themselves
probably why they cry—

girls get pregnant
men spit down drains
poems aren't so very different—
red domenico
ruffled cock in spanish courtyard
who the hell cares anyway—

art for art's sake
drains for drains' sake
girls for producing girls for producing girls for—

green green
go go go
i accelerate you accelerate they accelerate
we move forward

Place de la Contr' Escarpe

Walking through hours of narrow streets
in Miller's and Hemingway's Paris, we reached a square
enclosed by centuries sagged against each other:
homes that had stared out the Terror,
the Commune, Hitler, the rising of 'Sixty Eight.

In the tallest building a window suddenly opened,
a dark girl leant out and stayed there, singing;
not noticed by the women hobbling beneath,
their endless concern with how to make ends meet,
the students strolling arm-in-arm between
fresh lunges at sex, or arguing
interminably over coffee the bombs
of Vietnam, rank black injustices,
what others' lives their words could use to wrench
from humankind its frailty and strangeness.

Callanish

Two dwindling lovers run to the Standing Stones;
she, leaning against a slab's root, her full
breasts humping a thin summer frock;
he, crouching to fill his camera-spool
with the novelty of her smile. A wind to the sea spoke
shifting the loose weight from its sandy bones.

Safe enough now to pose in this rattled jaw
decay has weathered open; idly to prise
sheep droppings, birds' feathers, a rabbit skull aside
from the teeth stumped blunt by want of sacrifice,
earth having now more varied deaths to bride.
Once, an expectant breath of people saw

blindfolded boys and virgins forced to lean
bared throats to waiting vessels; felt the scream
fix to each draining face, their heated blood
invoke dark sleep from seed and semen, teem
with sap whatever multiplied, make good
thin fields and beasts' and women's wombs, between

one hunger and the next. The lovers rise, move off,
unnoticed minutes from their slip of time
dripped to the rimless vessel of what's passed
that chills all human blood; only the rime
of silence against silence left at last
to distance and the shrugging sea's cough.

The Devil's Elbow

Driving northwards through the dusk,
the car lights were blocked by banks of mist
exhaling thyme and heather. They'd unbent
another hairpin when the wire of the road
was suddenly furred with rabbits. Swerve or brake,
you couldn't avoid them. You could only sense
the unprotesting burst of their bodies.

Stop it! I hate you! For Christ's sake stop it!,
the girl in the passenger seat cried,
as if it was someone's fault; as if one could simply
stop at half-way nowhere. The wheels turned off
the small stains. A singer of heroic
suffering, of deaths larger than life,
sat sobbing in the steady purr of the car
taking her to the place of her next engagement.

Blow-up

They led the leader out to his execution
wearing a hat against the heat of the sun.
He stood backed to a wall wearing the hat,
the flush of unappreciated efforts
on behalf of his people, and (of course) himself,
drained from his bandaged face. At a given signal
a row of rifles spurted, the hat jumped
clean into the air, a fat body
shrank; a cheer ballooned, coloured with windy
slogans, airs of humanity and justice.
Soldiers tossed a body onto a truck;
humanity and justice thinned, deflated
for the time being, leaving behind a pool
of blood, a hat upturned to the sun.

An Elegy
(Matthew Lindsay: 1884–1969)

You might have died so many kinds of death
as you drove yourself through eighty-four Novembers—

1916. The Cameronian officer
keeping the Lewis gun he commanded chattering
over the seething mud, that the enemy
should be told only in terms of bulky bodies,
for which oak leaves, a mention in dispatches.

1918. The fragment of a shell
leaving one side of a jaw and no speech,
the bone graft from the hip, Shakespeare mouthed
(most of the others asserting silences)
over and over again, till the old words
shaped themselves into audibility.

1921. An eighty-per-cent
disability pension, fifty the limit of life
expectancy, a determination of courage
that framed the public man, the ready maker
of witty dinner speeches, the League of Nations,
the benefits of insurance, the private man
shut in his nightly study, unapproachable,
sufficient leader of sporting tournaments,
debates and the placing of goodwill greetings in clubs.

1935. Now safely past
the doctors' prophecies. Four children, a popular
outward man wearing maturity,
top of his business tree, when the sap falters
and the soon-to-be again confounded doctors
pronounce a world-wide cruise the only hope,
not knowing hope was all he ever needed
or counted on to have to reckon with.

1940 to 50. Wartime fears
not for himself but for his family,
the public disappointments and the private
disasters written off with stock quotations
from Shakespeare or Fitzgerald, perhaps to prove
the well-known commonness of experience,
the enemy across the mud, old age.

1959. It was necessary
at seventy-five, to show he couldn't be taken
by enfilading weaknesses. A horse
raised his defiance up. It threw him merely
to Russia on a stretcher, with two sticks
to lean beginner's Russian upon.

1969. The end of a decade
of surgeons, paling blindness, heart attacks,
all beaten with familiar literature
bent into philosophic platitudes,
to the January day in his dressing-gown
when he sat recording plans for a last Burns Supper.

You might have died so many kinds of death
as you drove yourself through eighty-four Novembers
till you fell from your bed, apologised for such foolishness,
and from your sleep rode out where no man goes.

Toward Light

The distant fog-horns bicker, the near ones boom;
light bats across the ceiling of the room
where, forty years ago, I watched, awake;
a still unfocused schoolboy out to take
life by the meaning. Then, the mist that gripped
the perfumed garden, kept the sea tight-lipped,
hung vague on sheltering curtains; the boy's mind
compassed on ships whose fogs lay far behind.
Now, with the frame loose, the window bare,
a blunt beam's thrown back on its own stare.

To Hugh MacDiarmid
(on his seventy-fifth birthday)

You rang the great bells of our Celtic hills.
The ageless sound you shook from them so fills
the Lowland plains and valleys that divide
silence from silence, no place now may hide
meanness of spirit; for it must be seen
in the clear singing light that you have been,
a huge integrity that gave despair
no shelter for its shadow anywhere.

The wholeness that you sought eluded you,
the ultimate good, the absolute, the true.
The very size and nature of your theme
meant you could never hold and fix the dream.
Though waters turn, the stream divides again,
and different problems baffle different men,
your challenge and your music leave behind
another Scotland those ahead must find:
for you have changed our climate of the mind.

V

Poems from *Walking Without an Overcoat* (1977),
Collected Poems (1979)

How Do You Do?

I push a trolley through the supermarket
every Saturday morning. Pears and apples
cry winds among the grasses. Potatoes
flaunt their smell of earth.
Oranges mimic fallen suns.
Meat glistens, cut square or minced
to help make sure it can't suggest
the breathing thing it came from. Battered fish
fingers hold on to lower prices.

Now and then I say to myself—
In this glad day of advertisers' tidings,
of open shelves stacked with full processes,
of ripping cellophane and throwaway,
it's wrong to hide inside a symphony,
skulk between painterly abstractions.

So every Saturday morning I push a trolley
through the supermarket. Other trollies
bump against mine. Disguised extractors
keep the air fresh for humans. Concealed intracators
puff the sound of music; sentimental
love that can't undo its packaged fancies;
a tune of Mozart's forced back on itself
inanely; moans and grunts of those who couldn't
make out on sex flipped up on making money.

My next week's intake duly recorded
by the electric register, the tally
unwinding like a toilet-roll, I store
the boot of my car, drive home
to my imagination, and write a poem.

For Pity's Sake!

People over fifty have no relevance,
said Tickybot This or That, the newest trendy.

What a surprise! I wondered where I'd lost mine.
Could they have clipped it out with my appendix,
by-passed it, like the way they fixed my ulcer?
Funny I hadn't noticed, though. Or had it
rubbed off upon the flesh of all my loving?
Or could the damp light of our northern skies
have mucosed it to thick monotony:
thinned it with customary wind and rain:
experience used it bare, like silver plating?

At first it had me worried, till I noticed
the poetry of people trapped by violence,
rape, mindless prejudice, cupidity,
shut up for saying what they think or see,
was still recording, syllabled with pity
to stay my whole subtraction from myself.

Then the thought struck me: *How could Tickybot know,*
with thirty years of relevance to go?

Poet

Red Sea, Dead Sea, Black Sea, Blue Danube—
romantic designations, disappointments.

I choose the white sea, paper. Here,
I flick the mind's lines with baited pen.

People ask me why. It doesn't pay.
I'm lonely. I get stung with withered grasses.

But I keep casting, now and then unhooking
wonder or pity off a bent hope.

Disused Canal

Stagnated mud oozed dank water
from backyard factories and mills,
where railway tunnels trickled rust
to what ran clean from distant hills.

Crooked in shallow clutches, froth
rubbed against a sedgy bank.
Discarded sheaths, a soleless shoe,
cartons unshaped by dampness, stank

of tomcat's piss. Bent railings gapped
on pressed-down gravel, while the drench
of rain on poverty and stone
flaking decay gave off its stench.

Kids who had nowhere safe to play
acted the fantasies they'd learned
on TV, getting nothing else
from parents who had never earned.

One small defeated Indian plunged
a headlong hole through grassy scum.
He made more noise, a cowboy said,
than those blind pups thrown in by Mum.

Children that age, the inquest heard
a distant grey-voiced man declare,
are not responsible in law
and must be taken into care.

A priest pronounced his hired refrain;
a pregnant belly slewed from prayer,
thankful the Blessed Virgin's gain
would leave the others more to share,
While an unlucky thirteenth child
emptied its littleness on air.

After the Game

He never topped any classes,
or aimed to be a shop steward
loud with demand; or boss masses
with ranting promise. He was just
an ordinary boy; somebody's
son, who liked football; saw
things fairly, through glasses.

Nobody ever quite knew
why it should have been him they picked on,
gobbed aim for oaths and spittle,
cringed beneath a swell of blows.

At first he pawed circled ground,
fumbling after dropped sight,
sweat on animal faces tense
as bruised fingers almost found
the broken frame. To cries of *shite*,
cackling heels crunched the lenses.

Somewhere behind, a dustbin clattered:
careful people steered clear
on the other side of the street.
I say, one passer-by kept saying
edged high on helpless conscience.

Out of a sound of running feet
a muscular priest charged to punch
original sin. Shouldered louts
shoved him back, *fuck off,*
you cuntless prick ringing his ears
as he ran to the nearest telephone,
his God-line trailing in arrears.

There wasn't much the police could do.
Their story to the press withheld
his name, till they told the next-of-kin.

Outings

I watched them rolling up to pray
in cars and furs; no doubt to say
how much they valued rounded health,
perhaps some thank-you for their wealth,
strength to withstand a scheming boss,
or solace for a heart-felt loss,
prayers as are made to be received
with neither man nor God deceived.

But from a nearby spastics' home
a woman and her creature come;
half-featured, dropped in spoiling haste;
it grips its mother's thickened waist
and grunts. She smiles, by now aware
such groped affection's all its share,
and nothing anyone can do—
not her, their prayed-at God, or you.

Only Connect

Daylight slackened city buildings;
streets filled with tension; through
all variations of direction
a crowd discharged itself,
counter-flows of energy re-shaping
to family groups round telly,
drinkers islanded in glasses,
lovers handling love, boredoms
deafened by their own silence.

One man hung out, the loose connection,
his covering of clothes frayed, his
circuit of cleanliness broken down:
one in whom a fault had developed
no specialist could diagnose.
His shambling despair discharged
momentarily against me.
Thruppence for a cup of tea.
the strawy lair-smell shuffled.

I gave him what he asked, knowing
it wasn't what he needed; knowing
nothing could do up the wrong
those dumb, bewildered eyes pleaded:
then hurriedly bought an evening paper,
and rushed to catch my waiting train.

Summer Sales

LESS LUST
LESS PASSION
FOR THE HEALTHIER LIFE
EAT NUTS

A scarecrow of a man proclaimed
in sunny, lunchtime Oxford Street,
balancing the poster-pole
on words half-murmured to himself.

Fixed in expansive summer, women
lusting after any bargains
focused their astonishment,
ranging the stare that fixed his face.
Lovers, propping passion on
each other's arms, smiled disbelief.
Blimey! He thinks we're monkeys! Laughter.

An unimpassioned constable,
his lust contained in uniform
of measured tread, came pacing in.
Move on, he said; *you can't stop here* . . .
(as if the man were anywhere)
Get moving. Come now. On your way.

The man moved on. But, as he passed,
I heard his toneless whispering.
John Smith, John Smith, John Smith, John Smith;
a lost voice crying its own name.

Dusk in a Glasgow Square

Darkness obliterates. Round arcs of light
the street lamps probe dried leaves. Their naked rustle
edges decay against the smell of night.
Kerbing low-geared, a cruise of cars hustle
each other round an empty office block
to pull up when the flash of booted thighs
flickers. A shadow peels out from the flock
leaning her whispered offer. The driver buys,
and revs off to the nearest parking lot.
Crouched in the crumpled scuffle of a seat,
he satisfies the need he thinks he's bought,
then runs her freshly back to her old beat.

Some father re-adjusts the suit of his disguises;
some daughter finds again that men hold no surprises.

The Word Made Flesh

I switched off my car by two petrol pumps.
A bell didn't work, and a couple of thumps
on the door of the house brought no ready supplier
to answer the needs of a would-be buyer,
who hadn't the unrolled miles in his tank
to get anywhere near the ferried bank
that once kept godless money away
from worshipping crofters each seventh day.
The sea sat smiling, the wind went pooh,
as I wondered whatever on earth to do.
Then, just as a munching cow let plop
what it couldn't contain, I felt the drop
of a well-placed sanctimonious cough,
so precisely blamed that you couldn't scoff.
A minister, like the hoodiecrow
the Bible got bound with long ago,
had landed beside me. From where he came's
a guess-at for one of your telly games.

A bellying cloud, he swelled his brood
of scriptural thunders where he stood.
Damned limb of Satan, why this vain noise
to disturb the Sabbath? I swung surprise
in every accused direction to see
what he meant; then realised it was me.
But, sir (always courteous to the dead–
in–life) I politely said:
There's evidence in the gospels to show
Jesus did things on Sundays. We know
it from Matthew, Mark, Luke and John,
whom surely you can rely upon?
He held to his ground with a fixing stare:
Of that I am perfectly well aware.
But if Jesus Christ lived to-day in Skye,
such unchristian conduct wouldn't get by!

Two Weddings

The organ–sound reverberates
distantly through the Burne-Jones gloom
they pledged their bodies in. Time waits,
along with nervous bride and 'groom,
beside the door for friends to freeze
the ending of their separateness,
the fumble of a passing breeze
fondling his hair, rumpling her dress.

There's reassurance in his hand
as off they go to face each guest,
speeches and telegrams; then land,
alone at last, two pasts undressed
awkwardly to explore the skill
of making love, prepay the debt
each owes to each if they'd fulfil
the eager flesh's ageless fret.

It's thirty years since we two stood
beneath that arch; were sheared away
to ride through every veer of mood
poems and music raise from clay;
then learnt love's best accomplishment
let daily touching presence stray
us gently into shared content.
Reach safely there who leave to-day.

Late Summer

I watch you lie, relaxed on the warm grass
that patterns your contented body, the creak
of crickets and a slow bird-trill the wake
of summer. Syllables of cloud pass
darkened whispers over colours; flowers
lazily gaze, scenting each loosened breeze
that nudges stillness out of its own ease
to herd up shadows into flocks of showers:
while I, whose fingers recently undressed
years of our bedded habit, eagerly laid
my love on yours till we together made
a moment of the world and time possessed,
sunning in gratitude, like you lie spent,
hands laced as if to catch the wonder lent.

Milk

Slats of a worn door
let in sunlight and mice;
shadows dapple a floor
cobbled with daily use.

Here, there's no cause to think.
A woman patiently bends
cheek to steaming flank.
Life's at its old amends.

Coaxed by accustomed hands
milk spurts from udder to pail,
human to creature bound
by its soft female smell.

If there were another coming
of myth to bind our earth,
surely it would be homing
on this white flow of birth?

Roots

I brought a water-pitcher up from Spain,
guarding it on the 'plane
between my feet. It looked like shaped rest,
curves that much living-with had stressed
skin-brown; a woman's breasts, full gourdes
cool with what darkness hoards.

I've brought it to a lean and hating town,
to set it in the stillness of a room
where love is made; moistened, raised out of clay
to which alike, one day,
pitcher and flesh must both again go down.

Poacher's Moon

A boat edged to shore,
darkness slapping her prow,
the phosphorescent oars
feathered gently to nudge
her ride on gravel's crunch.

Pulled up, her humphed keel
rasped pebbles. She lay
half on her black side,
dry out of water's reach.

Shadows gathered things
out of a move of talk;
sea-boots, an empty flask,
fish strung by the gills;
and then began to joke
homeward to female warmth;
roughened, familiar hands
well used to any catch.

Gale Force

Girning, whining sea;
bullying, thumping sea;
grinder of teeth, old white-hairer roarer:
how you run before the wind!

Missing Out

It comes to us all, the man said, sooner or later;
in your case, I'm afraid, sooner. But we're grateful
for all you've done for the Company, and wish you
a happy retirement.

Every day he walked to the skin's-edge
of land and sea to watch a needed happening,
and stood there by the same yard of sand,
the intercourse of wind and waves, for the moment
done with archetypal argument.

Every day he stood there, raincoat
flapping, while corpulent dippers
with no warm south to fly to, peeped and pittered,
footprints pointing back to where they'd come from,
absence of places which they couldn't notice
secure in their uncertain element.

Rush-hour Happening

If you Love Jesus or Would Turn to God
Honk—said the stickered car, under red lights.
So elevated were its driver's sights
he groped for leaflets while the traffic sawed
its sideways arm across the waiting queue.
Next to me, caged, a bulging driver stared,
cursed behind silent glass, then leaning, blared
the honk that Jerichoan trumpets blew.
Leaflet in hand, the holy freaker smiled,
leapt deep into a swerve of passing bus;
Oh sir, I'm truly glad you're one of us!
The gift of wonder opened by a child;
but heaven's never what we think we've seen.
For Christ's sake, get to your car! The light's at green.

Romantics

Leaves as red as rowanberries ride
the wind on the far side of the western wood.
They drain their colour into the dun mould
that squelches Autumn over half the road
where tractors stutter in and out of fields
lifting the last of what the season yields.

That smell twitches the flanks of memory.
Again I'm a boy, easy on speaking terms
with growing things, and a wide spank of sky
cold, then as now, with what the late year turns.
Clusters of hoof-beats tumble the trailed air,
swept up by hounds; a shout of huntsmen flare

out from the trees, leaving a lingering
of horses' sweat among the branches; a theme
for prancing horns, a centuries-young king,
royal as ballet, leading everything.
What follows is a small tongue-hanging stare
limping its breath back to a sundered lair.

Animals

Driving into the country at first light
after the occupation has withdrawn,
cornfields re-position the unfenced roads,
but casualties lie scattered all along;

here, three hedgehogs, each a moccasin
of needles stitching back the flattened pelt;
there, a dressing of crow's feather's, left
as if the bird had flown out of itself;
a cat drips the wound of its ninth life;
a hare's entrails glisten, newly surprised
out of its bounds; a dog's jaw gapes
with disbelief it never realised.

Driving through a world where they also kill
for kicks and causes, I wonder: *How many more undone
by mindless fingering?*, switch the radio on,
and leave these lesser litanies to the decent sun.

Uprooted

Straining against a winter's day
that wind got up to lift the sea.
It clutched at straws from shaking air,
it whistled courage to the shore.
Lurching defeated, with a crack
it laid an elm-tree on its back
from pointing twelve to levelled three,
its shadows folding disarray.

There used to be an old saying
when these things were worth the knowing;
Safe as houses, tall as trees.
Such were a boy's securities;
the elm-tree's polished knuckle-roots,
the earth's firm bones beneath his boots.
But random bomb and robbing gale
have shown there's nothing chance won't sell.

Where lovers once explored their shades,
white dust screams from biting blades;
blunt axes hack the scattered shape;
and from a chancer-man I take
the price of logs; a loaded cart
to burn up hunks of resined hurt.
Absurd, I say, and pick a book;
but what I read is branching smoke.

Disused Railway

The railway meanders through abandoned brickworks.
Severed by trunk roads and a housing scheme
it straggles disconnection through those meadows
it greeted once with daily shouts of steam.
Here and there farm palings run, bisecting
the down-line signalled readiness. Rusty tracks
lean emptily round curves no one's inspecting
but curious ramblers humping urban packs.
Soon this line will be half-forgotten rumour,
a shape of use with human purpose gone,
like vitrified fort or wooded burial tumour
cattle and birds and grass claim as their own.
Meanwhile, on platforms that have lost their names,
bushes thrust up and fireweed spreads its flames.

Between the Play and the Party
Political Broadcast

Punctually at home every evening
a pink face stalked on a coloured tie
defines for us the latest in violence;
there are always new ways for men to die.

Sometimes he brings it packaged; the larger size
an earthquake, 'plane disaster, lava flow;
the smaller, a kidnapping, multiple car-crash;
we're not to blame, and everyone must go.

Sometimes unwrapped; a soldier shot on a corner;
an old man battered sleeping on his bed;
a girl raped and choked behind a hedgerow;
one thing in common, all of them are dead.

Wearing the shadow in which we dress up pity
seemly to walk us through the long enduring,
where now's our vanquished hurt of youth, with its naked
constant apocalypse of hopeless caring?

Policy Committee

After dinner twelve men sit talking,
each accompanied only by his own importance,
misted in cigarette smoke, the smell of cigars.
They are formulating plans for the future
amongst the crumbs of broken bread, the dregs
of wine, impersonal as shed blood,
glinting from guttered candles. Spilled faces
pouched together over secret failures
too numerous for a private importance to
make public mention of. They blur
on possibilities of limited break-through;
on how to keep a united Party behind them;
on different ways of being mostly wrong.

While this goes on,
in countless indefinable ways
the future is planning itself to happen.

By Central Park, New York

He tightened his grip on the ornamental railings.
Whatever was happening, he had to hold on.
Through leaf-shaped holes he gazed up at the greenness
of trees waving *goodbye, goodbye, goodbye*
to each direction anything was taking,
all of those trees the same tree, sleeves of shadow
slapping his face, too late for challenging.

Couldn't everyone see what was happening?
That boy and girl there, under the lowest branches;
children at tig, turned to lovers, printing
flesh upon flesh, their dying faces
sapless as leaves crushed down by touching children?

Couldn't they see; the changing, changeless faces,
in the twinkling of an eye, corruptible?
Birth, copulation, death: beneath the thudding
sky's blueness, heaving thighs of cloud
that trees stood up and mimicked, stripping, dressing
women merged inside the maze of his senses . . .
Christ! He's blown to death, a cradling waft
of bosom absolved him. Space fell out the railings.

Sightseeing, Philadelphia

It was to have been a purely routine visit . . .

The mother of her estranged husband, Poles
apart, they had ganged language against her.
But she found the old woman dying, mother's darling
fled, unable to face the old one's subtraction
as he had failed the young one's loving body.
Don't let me go, the old one gasped. *Don't leave me.*
Don't let them . . . as four nurses moved to open
the cancer gap with a tubeful of meaningless air.

Men with vacant faces lazily spiked
litter and leaves from square to receptacles.
I sat on a bench, her biography of tears
telling its hurt to the clothes of a once-met stranger
she'd offered to show the town to.

                         Negresses,
bottoms stepped by high heels, nipples flaunting
bra–less sweaters, swaggered at corner-takers.
Under a tree, two mongrels copulated.

I sat on a bench, face brushed by sering leaves,
holding the hand of a prim librarian
who wept on my available shoulder; wept
humanity's confusion.

               Pigeons jerked
their puffy sheen, or necked available crumbs;
squirrels lolloped nuts, were shadows traced by
the question-mark of their tails up available trees;
all of us framed in a wheeze of anonymous traffic.

It was to have been a purely routine visit . . .

Winter Weekend, New Jersey

That evening got used up with argument;
just how the world might end; on what to think
of youth that needed pot to get it sent;
of middle-age spread out before the shrink;
puzzlement we'd none of us accept;
        nothing's for keeps, or kept.

That night, it felt as if the sky had shrunk.
The skin of darkness burst, and silence fell
white over churches, homes, the distant clank
of ceaseless factory yards. You couldn't tell
where the road went to, feathered among trees
        mimicking Christmases.

Being Sunday, the morning filled with prayer
for private lusts, great needs or valencies,
although it seemed the heavens lay scattered there,
disposed in weightless cold equalities;
each personal god stripped to a naked light;
        visible through blue-white.

Yet even as we stared, a frozen branch
squeezed out its glazed snow-shadow, like a sponge
dripping; a nowhere bird took off on chance
that soon a somehow wind would rise and plunge
the shapes of difference back to earth's wet ways,
        whose transience is praise.

Chicago Bookshop

Row upon row of cheaply bound-up facts;
how a machine performs, a species acts;
how to avoid disease, a damaged heart
or, having got one, make a new half-start;
how to relieve the weight of business stress;
psychiatry for each emotion's mess;
safe petting; marriage; coaxing more from sex;
divorce; re-marriage so that you won't vex
the children; even, gracefully how to die.
Here's living's ready reckoned *How?* and *Why?*—
except for happiness, not a bargain buy.

On Milton Hill

Since I moved up to live among the birds,
gathering round my house their shawl of woods,
trees have turned staves where notes and dotted wings
measure the movements each new season brings,
phrasing the round of fields and sky, the moods
that seas and clouds whip up, or fleck like curds.

The blackbird scoops the robin's worm; the thrush
parades stout elegance like admiration;
the dusty sparrow's fussed with small concerns;
the cuckoo clarinets dropped thirds. We learn
a watching metaphor of situation
that seems to match the ways of house and bush.

But here's distorting; a reflection of our kind's
desire to settle always within reason.
We must take this realm of birds we can't possess
on its own terms; let wonder re-confess
uncertainties no dogmatist can seize on,
flaring its fresh delights time out of mind.

Milton Hill

The heat comes in out of the blue,
shimmering clear, like water seen through;
lapping at shadows, glistening leaves
with beaded moisture. Distant traffic sieves
its glinting hum through liquid haziness
while small birds cheep their local laziness.
Between, the silty channel of the Clyde,
a spill of silver, bronzed at either side,
where trains pick up then drop their *dickety-dack*
through fields of cows munching their shadows back;
behind, a squirrel flows from stone to stone
making a wall seem rippling on its own;
idled on drowsiness I lie,
half-wondering what's to pay for such clear sky.

On the Balcony

The summer day wore down to a cool evening.
I had locked up the lumber of my mind
to loll upon a balcony. A ship's
outline shivered the narrow Clyde through hills
already blue with gathered distance. Suddenly
swallows like moving shadows pivotted,
zigging a voltage from Italian skies,
wiring our Northern air. And watching, I
experienced a shapeless happiness.
Not *good* or *bad*, or any other kind
of categoried looking-glass hung there;
rather it was as if I'd somehow strolled
into the heat and centre of time's moment
and overlooked my whole self unawares.

999

Is that the Fire Brigade?

Yes, the Fire Brigade.

Where's the fire?

There isn't a fire. It's water.

Water?

Yes, water. Coming through the roof in seventeen places.
We're being flooded. Please can you come and help us?
A waterfall. It's pouring down the stairs like Niagara.
What's fallen?

Water.

But we're the Fire Brigade.

I know you're the Fire Brigade. But I've seen on the telly
rescuing flooded-out people with boats. *Yes, we do that.*
But you're at the top of a hill. You can't get boats there.
I know you can't. But, I tell you, we're being flooded.
We need your help. *If it isn't a case for boats, then*
I'll speak to the Superintendent and ring you back . . .

. . . Is that the Fire Brigade ringing back?

Yes, the Fire Brigade.

Are you coming to help?

Well, no, I'm afraid we're not.
If your cat got stuck up a tree, or the dog on the roof,
or, of course, you'd an actual fire . . .

I'll put him there.

Put who where?

The dog on the roof.

Oh, you can't do that!
He'd have to get there by himself. What the hell's that noise?
I'm sticking the cat up a . . .

Look, you'd better get off
the line, chum. Some folk's maybe in serious trouble.

Tailpiece

(In the Rotary Tools trial of 1976, Mrs Grant, according to popular report, was erroneously
referred to through the proceedings as Mrs Grunt.)

O Muse! Some special strength may I be lunt
to sing an *a* that opened up to *u*,
and left a married woman in the stew:
an upright legal tale that should enchunt.
Her cuddly-teddy boss set up the stant.
Nothing was said. Between inviting thighs
tired customers released their free surprise
that tools move readier through accustomed cant.
Corruption's hound was loosed upon the hant:
the victims cringed before its scorching punt.
From careless stroke of pen, what virtue's bunt?
What credit's robbed from an industrious frant?
But could the law's impartial truth have munt
to keep poor Anita's grant, forever grunt?

Between Two Worlds

Every morning at nine, past my window
Woofles, the affectionate Persian cat,
creeps along the line of his own balance
paw upon paw, as if afraid of his weight.

Known only to Woofles, the line stretches through
a hole in the dyke, into the wood beyond,
where mice flicker like leaves, and baby rabbits
listen, as if by their own foolishness stunned.

There's nothing to hear, except the blundered dog
barking at distance that it can't leap through
to leave the pampered time of humans. Meanwhile,
the line's run out as far as it need go.

Mouse or baby rabbit never knows
what the pounce came from. Scuffle or squeak
as instant wills, the yellow eyes burn,
the teeth rend and crunch, the small bones break.

Having rolled up the slackened line on whiskers
scentlessly clean, a jump back out of his skulk,
and there, without a hint of blood still warm,
is pussy, round your ankles after milk.

Mongrel

There was a hi-jack, and a pop-star died
of self-indulgence. Politicians lied
to an investigating jury. Good and bad
men everywhere got murdered. The usual sad
day, should you be rash enough to think
of it. Except that from a swirling chink
of Glasgow fog, a black dog padded through
abandoned isolation. *Yes, you'll do, . . .*
his questioning tail and panting tongue proclaimed.
Woozy, this wag of energy was named.

He cut a dash of eager agitation
in search of dumb uncoloured information
about the human world he breathily loved,
wriggling affection till he was approved.
Wherever water gathered, he would swim,
his fur a forest shadow, nose a skim
of movement. Tracing miles of hidden scent,
he'd keep unearthing primitive content,
beyond the reach of our bewilderment.

As men are dropped from life before their time,
this dog was clawed by cancer in its prime;
and on the day it slipped to whence it came,
six terrorists crept out to kill or maim;
a child of five drowned in a shallow pool,
held under as it made its way from school;
while holy men ran up their prayers again
to shake the silent God of human shame.

A dog was dead, an ordinary day
compost upon the heap of history.

Glasgow Orange Walk

Walking with my daughter to her wedding,
murder came marching through the town;
two thin ranks of policemen stayed it
from coming into its own.
Spread women, ugly men and little children
dressed in the Sunday best of bigotry,
suffered to come unto intolerance
down orange miles of bannered frippery;
the gadfly flutes, the goading fifes,
the yattering side-drums of expended wars
forcing sectarian division through
our public streets choked back with fuming cars.

Between one section's end and the next,
led by a white-gloved prancer with a stick—
a clown without true clowning's dignity—
we seized our chance to get there. I said *Quick:*
and we were through.

        A piece of the thing
leapt at us, a bulge of animal red,
knuckles half-raised, *D'ya waant tae get fuckanwell killed?*
'Back now. Get back,' a policeman intervened;
the threat retreated and the rite re-filled,
folded by blue mackintoshes, held
to keep democracy safe for those who hate
for the Queen's fame, in the name of Jesus.

Les Eyzies

We warmed our patience in the sun,
tourists in shorts, the tall and curious;
school-children out to learn perspectives
between licks of ice-cream;
cyclists with coffee-flasks and buns,
munching delay till their turn came for seeing
what guide-books had so set their minds upon.
Not to waste time among rocks
older than unimaginable years,
a pale unshaven Cambridge don
lectured on concepts to his girl.

Picking our way at last, cautious and slow,
into an opened cleft that moulded more
than all the Sabbaths men have fashioned,
a fitting torch that pointed in neat French
what scholarly researchers said,
guided us through the heartfelt prayers
of thirty thousand years ago
painted on stone: the bison's shouldered threat,
muscled and tensed, about to hurl
himself at cave-man's fears
hungered to kill, before that thundering charge
scattered the cunning of his flinty spears.

Blinking the little light of our own times,
I tried to visualise that length of frieze,
kept sealed from man's corrupting argument—
Christ an already fading yesterday,
Europe's revolutions minutes done—
and felt strange love for our inconsequence:
tourists in shorts, now queuing up for postcards
to fix their memories; cyclists pedalling
towards further destinations; children wearing down
their ice-cream pleasure mountains,
the Cambridge don still lecturing on concepts,
unpeopled earth our past and prophecy.

A Minister of Religion

Farewell, kind-hearted dogmatising friend,
who undervalued 'life on earth below'
in hope of 'lasting glories' at the end.
If right, you're there at heaven's non-stop show,
waiting to greet me—*See! It's all I claimed.* . . .
Pity you never got your doubting tamed—
as, ticketless, I'm ushered down below.
If wrong—why, neither of us will ever know!

Lifestyles

Stop the world, I want to get off, the comedian sang;
I guess we'll have to tough it, the politician lied;
Strike, or you'll never work again, the shop-steward cried;
Smash the bugger's face in, snivelled the teen-age gang;
Turn to the God of your fathers, an empty voice rang;
Work, worry and rain once more, the bored one sighed;
The State can bloody pay, sniffed one who'd never tried;
What we all need's a leader who'll make the wicked hang!

Must we always herd for cover, cringe at blame,
let violence roam large, the buried ape
unwind the wonder of us, man and woman,
complain that each day's newness is the same,
or pray to air, to find we can't escape
the responsibility of being human?

Dans la Piscine

However much our expectations hone us,
we can't predict when life declares a bonus:
these *Glorias* described by holy men,
nothings that tremble on their edge, and then
sink back into the rounded drone of praise
the rest of us think ordinary days.

A brief bikini by an open pool,
teaching a splash of youngsters swimming's rule,
her hair, her neck, her settled mien, her face
what sinful men conceive the look of grace;
the lift of her breasts, her belly's gentle curve,
a skin that rippled litheness with each move,
she stooped to her concerns, and seemed to be
the ripe perfection of virginity.

Swimming decades apart, I warmed to watch
her bend away and shape a cotton crotch
where some man's hand would kindle a new fire,
heating her to his own and time's desire.
Yet for a fitting moment, there she stands,
unplucked, with others' children on her hands,
as if unconscious of the flesh's need
for love to pull her down, and swell and breed.

How many *Hallelujahs* would you raise,
you holy men, for one such worshipped gaze!
I've had a cold shower in the best tradition
to keep my doubtful soul from your perdition,
and strop the towel of penance on your lack
of absolution, mopping up my back.

Concert

Stroking at strings to make a singing edge
or channelling their fingered breath through gauge
of ebony or brass, musicians play,
as if what they produced was workaday.
Tribally, the audience, unaware
it looks absurd, sits in a motionless stare—
till out of disappointments, hungers, aches
of body, self-tormenting fret, there wakes
the gift of love, a tremble of elation,
a sudden, strange fulfilling agitation,
some brief content not ours to have or hold
touching on meanings words must leave untold.

Conductors
(for Sir Alexander Gibson)

Words and the notes of music—meanings pointing
at distances we can't get to unaided
unless we are conducted. Dictionaries
define conduct as 'manage', 'guide', 'direct',
or 'serve as a channel'. We conduct ourselves
from face to face, and travel situations
we often wonder why we've reached. Conductors
in uniform are there for us to purchase
a piece of distance from, for us to use
with what the moment makes us think are reasons.
Tall buildings, brittle in their fixed importance,
conduct unbolted lightning straight to earth
by circumventing their own distances.
But above others most to be revered,
conductors of music; subtle channellers
who give life back itself, mind out of time,
sensing us with a brief imagined glory
that plays about our shabby human story.

Das Lied von der Erde

Roses have fallen, the flesh has lost its tune,
the sound of flutes silvers a chilling moon;
the glint of wine has soured upon the tongue;
riderless now the horsing seasons come;
gone are the firm of limb whose laughter kissed
the morning air with hope, the longing dusk
with traced desires. Now, as the scent of musk
fingers old graveyards, moulders thought from books,
and breathes its doubt on well-remembered looks,
Ewig . . . the music sighs, and brings us near
the silence those it folds on never hear.

Revisiting Innellan

Sheltered behind a rock a woman sits
keeping an eye on more than what she knits;
her hands the flashing motion of the sea,
veined with the dulse of vulnerability.

Gulls, stiff as saddles, ride the little bay
much as they rode the winds of yesterday.
A toy yacht arrows over shallow water
wafted by splashing knees and gusts of laughter.
The boy beside the pool lets down his hand
to guddle baby crabs from shifting sand.

The same reflected sky, the same blue shout
through which a bather plunges, and runs out,
his sticky skin rubbed dry with towelled grit,
a gravelly biscuit for his chittering bit.
Though different the clothes, the cut of ships,
the waves still curl those same contemptuous lips
that spit the wrack of winter up the beach,
lost purposes unshaped from human reach.

Watching alone, an old man nobody knows
catches inquiring looks, gets up and goes.

How Now, Prospero?

My ending is despair,
feigning no prayer
to offer to some god, man-made
so that it might be said.

VI

A Net to Catch the Winds (1981)
(A gratitudinal canter in light verse)

A Net to Catch the Winds
(For Joyce)

Whispered leaves and lovers kissing
gentleness there's no amassing,
music into silence tossing
     time rescinds.
Quick, poet, in the passing—
     a net to catch the winds!

1

Whatever fame you seek or rank aspire to,
or pleasures buy, conventional or odd,
there comes a moment when you can't conspire to
elasticate your tread from stiffened plod;
those weakened like Gerontius suspire to
the fancied shade of some constructed God
to spare their favoured souls oblivion's knife:
others, like me, just murmur: *Thank you, life!*

2

But gratitude's demands are more capacious
than to acquit a poet with one stanza,
his appetite for living still voracious.
What follows may in practice be just *sans* a
bare fact or two, but when the mode is spacious
wise readers know that poetry's bonanza
is never found constrained by what defines;
it's what emerges from between the lines.

3

Besides, throughout my life one keen ambition's
alone among the rest unsatisfied,
perhaps because my muse felt its conditions
too strict for any subject that she eyed,
doubting her rhymer's skill for such renditions:
throughout the years I've wished that I had tried
to write a poem in *otta rima*,
which, were I English, I would rhyme with *schemer.*

4

But I'm not English; I'm a Glasgow Scot
born in what's now a Conservation Area
where laws control what you may do, what not.
For instance, woe betide you if you vary a
weathered saint, or plaster faceless rot;
you must replace them, even if there's nary a
public penny's help when you restore
what puffs and peels off like an ageing whore.

5

Those distant years ago when I appeared there
the place was in its prime, or so I'm told,
Rolls-Royces multiplying as you neared there;
but cars, like whores, mean nothing one day old;
your mother's milk is all that you revered there,
or nappy change when it was wet and cold:
unless, like dear Mackenzie, your recalling's
so total you still hear your infant bawlings.

6

My bandaged father lay somewhere in France,
wounded to silence in the Kaiser's war.
My mother ripened in an anxious trance,
uncertain if he'd see the child she bore.
But he was master of unlucky chance;
work, golf and war were games where one could score.
They said by fifty he'd not be alive;
he talked his vigorous way to eighty-five.

7

An uncle substituted for my father;
through boyhood years I was to him a son.
Until he died I found that I'd much rather
the substitute had been the real one.
Each Saturday, together we'd forgather,
and go exploring through comparison.
From him I learned the texture of the ways
a city shapes its huge anonymous days.

8

The kind of learning that I got at school
seemed dull when, after lying on my tummy
in a friend's house, aged twelve, against the rule
up late, the radio, as usual, crummy,
half-slipping under drowsiness's pull,
I suddenly sat upright on my bum be-
cause Haydn's music had enlarged the air,
sending delightful shivers everywhere.

9

O music! after love my first of pleasures;
dear joy! worth application's sacrifice,
enriching beyond speech with strains and measures
to substance feeling when the action dies;
for me like breath, not just a taste for leisure,
the worship that I gave you proved unwise.
At French I flopped, in mathematics fumbled;
The boy won't concentrate, my teachers grumbled.

10

Two other sirens whispered at my side.
With words of daily contact, Poetry's muse
murmured in sounds that sent a softening tide
of feelings, which as yet I couldn't use,
through me; but feelings that I wouldn't hide.
These or hard facts? I knew I had to choose.
The senses won. I chose to follow art;
which seemed the richer way, money apart.

11

The second muse from puberty's horizon
took, not surprisingly, the shape of girl.
No doubt today you wouldn't put a prize on
the she who set my thoughts in such a whirl.
Month after month she kept her childish guise on;
some husband later plucked her virtue's pearl,
for Nature scarce allowed us more than kiss,
me thirteen, she a breastless twelve-year miss.

12

Throughout my days to one thing I've held steady;
women were never inches in a tape.
My mother grew alarmed, though, when I said I
preferred a violin's to the female shape;
that was, until I saw a naked lady:
(what wonders lie concealed beneath a drape!)
Such posing young men hold to gain effect—
a sign of undeveloped intellect.

13

Meanwhile I slaved, when not engaged in schooling.
For hours I tackled Rode, Kreutzer, Spohr.
While other boys indulged in sport or fooling
with ogling girls, alone I'd practise more
thirds, sixths, arpeggios, octaves, double trilling
until my neck and finger-tips grew sore.
Imaged in self-love poor Narcissus drowned;
verse-making kept my thoughts on firmer ground.

14

Each Spring, proclaimed by trumpets daffodilled
in the Botanic Gardens while the tram
turning the Byres Road corner shrieked and shrilled,
I walked with Pope and pondered why I am,
a question which no obvious answer filled
that didn't smack of philosophic sham:
then, copying caesura and sensation,
I learned the poet's craft by imitation.

15

How else? From all that's past, the long connection
we can't escape's the blood of every one of us,
that ageless and incurable infection.
Whatever sallow youth thinks he'll have done of us
to give society a new complexion,
he's stuck at once with every mother's son of us:
unless he's homosexual or a hermit,
his stamping flesh endorses history's permit.

16

Then followed years when I was a Romantic.
There's few of us escape this lush complaint
since *Sturm und Drang*, with melancholic antic,
made subjectivity a cureless taint;
but cynicism, at its best semantic,
suspects the substance underneath the paint.
As well proclaim a faith in racial purity
as count on objectivity for surety!

17

Horse-drawn cabs to parties, yellow fogs,
cranes—flattened question-marks—above the river
seen from my bedroom window, crackled logs
and sherried aunts at Christmas—me, a sliver
of my found later self—were winter's cogs
turning a summer that I wished forever.
A paddle-steamer frothed us to the coast,
and all my searching fancy valued most.

18

Innellan opened gates of paradise;
glittering seas, the flush of flowers, and lawns
that slanted green with light, and the small eyes
of clouds floating blue days as halcyon's
a timeless fable; ships that passed like sighs,
their trailing foam wavelets that breathed anons
when ship and throb of churning screw had faded
into those distances that purpose traded.

19

The Clyde, it's true, was sometimes closed by mist
that clutched and clumped the Highland hills together,
and rain that shook the trees with angry fist;
but we forget the rages of rough weather,
remembering how honeysuckle kissed
after fresh showers, the wet caress of heather.
Since Nature's our one source of human healing,
no wonder poets finds her so appealing!

20

But there now; I grow lyric, and digress.
The simple fact is, one can't live on scenery,
and men who calculate the more or less
of money, pour impatient scorn on greenery,
except, perhaps, when draped in halls to dress
up sales of work done by the local Deanery,
or Presbytery, if by chance your class
equates your superstitions with the mass.

21

One winter afternoon, walking a dog,
I climbed a hillock sloping off in scree.
A slip of gravel gave the beast a shog,
tumbling it downwards. By a stunted tree
it found its feet. Proud as a demagogue
it stood there watching as, on hand and knee,
I slithered past it, fracturing a scaefoid;
of doggy gratitude it was, I'd say, void.

22

That brought a tacit end to violin playing
and saved me fiddling in some third-rate band.
It saved me, too, from soldierly affraying—
a thing I doubted if my nerves could stand.
I heard a board of doctors sternly saying
what proved a most relieving reprimand:
Your right hand doesn't have its full mobility;
you lack the fighting man's complete agility.

23

I was, of course, no cowardly escaper,
having resigned myself to killing's chance;
now, I commanded only bits of paper
that balanced options, figures, facts and plans;
of others' deaths unwittingly a shaper,
saved from their hell by comic circumstance.
Few men aspire to die as martyred stoics.
Necessity's the mother of heroics.

24

But back again to love. My next attack of it
I suffered when a student with no money,
that sesame which gives a man the knack of it;
a pianist, sweet-faced, by temper sunny,
her play was such that once I'd seen the back of it,
my pricked idealism seemed quite funny.
She found dissecting sheep a better bet
than Mozart; so she married with a vet.

25

Lucky in love the third time (and I shout of it),
I've been a husband close on forty years,
and never once endured a serious doubt of it.
You marriage critics, lend your stereo ears;
things must be good in bed; but in or out of it
respectful gentleness is what adheres,
once urgent flesh consumes its passion's rage
if you would keep a glow against cold age.

26

When what's described as peace again returned
a trainee I became in colour printing.
My bosses rationed everything I learned,
at greater speed and riches always hinting.
Dissatisfied with what I did and earned,
I broke from business bonds and set off sprinting
at my own pace up sloping Mount Parnassus.
How fortunate I listen to de Lassus,

27

or once again I'd stumble for a rhyme!
Broadcasting, writing, music-criticising,
and making love and poetry, the time
went quickly by without me realising
how brief the leafing years we call our prime.
In middle age we take to agonising
when fledglings rough us up in raucous tone
no matter what we've done or promise shown;

28

a thing that Scotland's wee-ness makes unique.
You must be useless if they knew your father,
or 'kennt yir faither' if in Scots you'd speak,
no longer a rich thoughtful tongue, but rather
a broken *patois* practised by a clique
(it's odd how fact puts some folk in a lather!)
of poetasters who, with nought to say
exhale their feeble breath on its decay.

29

You'd almost think I thought such nonsense counted!
I knew three poets who could use Scots well.
MacDiarmid, on his wings of genius, mounted
the lyric heights, until he sought to spell
out praise for Communism. Then, much dunted,
his muse excused chopped prose and doggerel.
Who fought to break the Scots parochial cage
supported gunned suppression in old age.

30

Dear Goodsir Smith, who sang of drink and women,
a connoisseur of laughter, wit and art;
of Scotland's writers warmly the most human,
monied and monocled to play the part:
and Alexander Scott, who right on cue ran
the follies of our land beneath a scart
of witty epigram. But their successors!—
let's call them Lallans Inc, prefixed by Messrs.

31

A Scottish writer has a choice of tongues—
Scots, Gaelic, English which we mostly speak,
the other two the subject of ding-dongs
through *Scotsman* letters every second week,
as if there was some case of rights and wrongs
that angry argument could win or break.
It's not the tongue that matters, but what's said in it;
unless it's how you feel, you'll be found dead in it.

32

Write English, and they'll say that you're defeatist.
If faced with quality that quite surpasses,
they'll dub your witty imagery élitist
unless it echoes praise for leftish masses,
whose sense of judgement's never been the neatest,
their clichés roaring out like sounding brasses.
Reject such brays with dignified austerity;
true judgement's given only by posterity.

33

Besides, wise living means that when we taste it
we savour each sensation as it offers.
Our circled round's too wonderful to waste it,
however much in thankless youth we're scoffers.
Age fingers time more thinly, and we haste it
unless we linger over all it proffers:
the texture's brittler but the touch more fine,
the flavour summered deeper through the wine.

34

To wine, I must admit, I've long been partial;
our link of bliss with mythic ages gone.
Alas! for those its elixir makes martial;
who drink it, then can't bear to look upon
another without violence; a farce you'll
agree is best avoided, not outshone.
When wine, the gift of light, provokes aggression,
a smalling creature mirrors his recession.

35

It's puzzled me how Scotsmen, wrapped up thickly
in inarticulateness, or when boozy,
fall into forceful argument and quickly
go fucking this and fucking that, their floosy
a naked oath. It makes the sober sickly—
allowing too much drink leaves men less choosey!—
to hear the link of joy that's life's infinity
with violence thus placed in consanguinity.

36

Poor tolerance, a pity you're so boring
that poets never wing you out in odes
or hymns of praise empowered to send you soaring
in strains to deafen all the niggling goads
of anger, setting men and nations roaring
at those who follow unfamiliar codes!
In wordy brawling, whether one's just socked, or
been felled, you wait on call, their only doctor.

37

There's not a man but needs his fill of pleasure
as through this vale of tears he's forced to pedal,
though when he meets with matters he can't measure
his views mean nothing and he'd best not meddle;
yet when he treats of what he loves in leisure,
though other folk might think it fiddle-faddle,
he's found his secret path to human glory,
lending exultant meaning to his story.

38

Whose story? Once again, my lines have bounded
unfenced from what is meant to be their theme,
the story of my life. So, muse, be rounded
up quietly this purpose to redeem.
When Scotland's television first was founded
the studio lights from many a slanting beam
focused on me, explaining why those japers,
The Jolly Beggars, cut immortal capers.

39

I'd been to see a television high man
to say: *I want to do the TV thing.*
But being an administrative fly-man
he questioned: *What experience do you bring?*
None yet, said I. He sighed and countered: *Why man,
if we want you we'll give your 'phone a ring.*
Experience, I blurted, *comes through function.*
A paradox! he answered, smooth as unction.

40

I fumed and fretted at such bare stupidity,
for double-tongued excuses I abhor;
but he proved innocent of such cupidity.
To tell the truth I don't put too much store
on Gaelic Mods; but, treated with fluidity,
these Teuchters may not prove too big a bore.
Go up to Oban with a camera crew,
he said: *and then we'll see what you can do.*

41

So I began my years of interviewing,
a smiling bow-tie image in the box,
trimming the tales of others to my cueing
through subjects sober, gay or heterodox,
the muddied paths of fact and truth pursuing.
Pause now, if you are one of those who mocks
the media. A thirst for information's
a taste that's only quenched in western nations.

42

'Pursuing truth' seems slightly high-faluting!
Of sides, my father claimed, the truth had three;
A's, passionately held, proved convoluting
when laid against the same believed by C.
The third approach, for which there's no one rooting,
passes somewhere between, elusive B.
And yet TV, for all its violent crudity
can sometimes strip a lie to mental nudity.

43

When *What is truth?* impatient Pilate queried
and for an answer would not wait, no wonder.
Since time for us began our wits have wearied
to find it, and we've torn ourselves asunder
quarrelling over rigmaroles that varied
this god from that, and each another blunder;
yet deep in our duplicity there lies
the strange belief there's life beyond the skies.

44

There's instinct in us all to stay alive,
without a struggle never to succumb.
The power at which all holy men connive
wields mindless fear to keep the doubters dumb.
Eternal hope's but brute survival's drive,
and reaches back the dark from which we come.
There's not a word been heard from *there*, outside,
that parsons haven't dreamt, then deified.

45

While chasing such chimeras as we long for,
at least we may establish proven facts,
though rarely what a poet sings his song for.
Gusted by passions, some impromptu acts
until they're over seem worth doing wrong for.
But life's a shifting compromise of pacts;
we sell ourselves to hold defeats at bay
till unexcusing age sweeps all away.

46

Broadcasting kept life filtering through my fingers,
sampling the surface truth of many ways;
yet something of their added substance lingers,
leaving my heart a testament of praise;
not for heroics that Mancunian 'sing-gers'
proclaim wherever management best pays;
but hopes and fears expressed in such humility
you'd weep to hear the creak of their fragility.

47

The fame a face attracts is unconvincing,
its partial level cut across the knees.
I've told the young, and watching their inward wincing,
that television's just like canning peas,
or stamping parts in factories, or mincing
up meat for sausages. Neglect to please,
and you'll be superseded in a twinkling,
with not a friend to share your lonely drinking!

48

It's better far to write a single verse
that fifty years from now sets one heart aching
in sympathy with what the lines rehearse,
than share a pop star's psychedelic shaking
of mindless millions; or look out—what's worse?—
to watch your insincerity overtaking;
or find yourself unbuttoning public scandal
to give your name a marketable handle.

49

Some writers have a passion for variety,
claiming it's what our flesh and blood were made for,
the constant repetition of satiety.
But many of the lovelies that get laid for
such pleasures as they lend, find notoriety
a post-coital sadness better paid for;
so, baring grief and naked secrets, sell
their tale of twitchings to the *Sunday Yell*.

50

A lovely woman taking off her clothing's
delight to men; a glimpse of promised seas
to carry freights of bliss and soft supposings,
meeting the distance of a moment's ease.
The eager male, when he begins disposing
of socks and trousers and the need to please
assumes a kind of awkward comicality,
if such things may be judged by rationality.

51

Our sexual tastes come varied, like religion,
and I'm not one to prate morality,
or urge the lusty young to keep the fridge on,
as preachers beg the commonality
with vested interest to preserve a bridge on
the gulf from life to immortality:
but parsons peer through self-deluding mists;
I don't believe a future state exists.

52

Or that a god of any kind's worth knowing
who needs continual praise for what he's gifted,
while ministers remind him what he's doing,
or point direction favours might be shifted
(according to his will, since nothing's owing)
as if, from time to time, omnipotence drifted.
The nameless source of life we call creation's
what artists search for through their own sensations.

53

The public think creation's a commotion
that stirs and stumps us every waking hour
while inspiration's poured out like a lotion,
the frenzied gift of some ethereal power.
If there was much in that romantic notion,
poets would all stay thin, composers sour:
unceasing works of art are indigestible;
we must exist on something more comestible.

54

Reporting rapes and writing up disasters
to poets is a kind of muse-abuse,
and few who do it ever prove long lasters.
On radio and TV, with George Bruce—
our audiences were more discerning masters—
the present and the past we'd introduce,
tracing the settled heritage that shaped us
and probing where its energy escaped us.

55

A shadow that has lost its substance, feeling
as well supported as a verbless clause,
the Scottish spirit's been too long congealing
in banknotes, sour religion and thinned laws,
while round about, the busy world is dealing
in purposes that wear a living cause.
Though Scots pretend they long for devolution,
they vote unchanged the London constitution.

56

That frees them from the burden of decision,
allowing them complain when things go wrong,
noising abroad much paper-dart derision
to keep the fiction jollying along.
No matter how original their vision,
they're soon bought out by foreign firms more strong.
Since most by now accept their branch-line station,
why press dishonoured claims to be a nation?

57

One must stay positive, though Scotland's slipping
beyond retrieval to provincial status;
for what will not return it's no use weeping.
Mankind's long march goes on. It should elate us
that slowly fairer values are outstripping
those with which privilege could still negate us
if democratic rule became dictation,
to tyrant's or Trade Unions' subjugation.

58

It was, perhaps, as wild a piece of dreaming
to visualise a virile Scotland, free
to make its choices, as the thought that scheming
among globe-trotting statesmen could decree
a peaceful balance for the world's redeeming,
the universal, equal vis-à-vis.
Since history's the sum of spent confusion,
all human life must end in disillusion.

59

That need not be depressing if around us
the young, impatient as they watch us fail,
await their turn, from dreaming to confound us
as straightly as a hammer hits the nail.
They'll learn one day, perhaps before they ground us,
that we, too, strove to break the harsh entail
bonded in blood so distant we can't think of it
though nowhere near, as yet, the middle link of it.

60

There was a time I thought my muse forsook me,
her usual urgent voice quite hard to hear;
and much that I then wrote wore such a look, the
reviewers drubbed me for being far from clear.
Five further years of wooing her it took me
before the saucy jade would reappear;
but when she did, at last she hung her hat up,
and here and there some kindly critic sat up.

61

Yet what's a muse but a convention, hoary
with time; a useful way to blame another
should readers much dislike a poem or story.
Some poets find their muse a shrilling bother;
Burns found his Coila such a crashing bore, he
addressed her like some nagging Holy Mother.
Of technique if you've laid a good supply on,
a kind sub-conscious is what you rely on.

62

And yet it's hard to keep a poem in focus,
guiding it towards its proper destination;
with winning words a facile muse provokes us
to jostle like a crammed suburban station;
or vague with dampish sentiment, so soaks us
we're forced to do a drying operation;
destroy what we have laboured at thus vainly
and shape another poem with moves more gainly.

63

Why bother writing poetry? folk ask me
from time to time. *It doesn't make much money.*
Quite true. And shaping verses doesn't bask me
in that enriched acclaim men find most sunny.
The inner voice is urgent, and can task me
to shut myself in my own mental dunny
while others brazen on the frolicked beach
reserved for those whose fortune's in their reach.

64

If human life bears any kind of reason
we're bound to seek whatever we do best
and nourish it through each succeeding season
till both the flower and fruit are manifest.
To kill the gifts we're given is a treason
that never should allow our conscience rest;
nor must we wield the mutilating knife
though fashioned critics make self-doubting rife.

65

Besides, why cramp a poet when he's wound up?
Staccato stammerings in verse called free
are what most would-be versifiers sound up
who pay their own poetic licence fee;
exhausted words and nerveless clichés bound up
for Editors, first class delivery.
So long as I'm a poet in employment,
I see no reason to forgo enjoyment.

66

No more apologies for such digression!
Few lives, thank goodness, ever run to plan.
We're linked by little more than chance succession,
leaving us rearrange as best we can.
Those who believe they've souls maintain confession
disperses faults, like some forgiving fan,
leaving them free to err again tomorrow,
a form of consolation I can't borrow.

67

Life jolts us on. We need to wash our faces
and laugh at times. Mere philosophic platitudes
never excuse us from those daily paces
that mete out disappointments and beatitudes.
Leaving elected men in public places
to strike up further unconvincing attitudes,
we eat, earn, spend, make love and all the rest,
ignore the worst by hoping for the best.

68

I left George Bruce (who made the North-East speak
its poetry of stone) and for a while
towards advertising turned a gentle cheek.
A television station in Carlisle
became my programmed care, and week by week
I broadcast from this city lacking style,
and longed to be in Scotland. I can't think why;
there only were ten English miles to slink by!

69

After six years, patched by an operation,
some programmes worth the doing left behind,
I felt the rub of alien frustration.
Against the English I've no axe to grind,
but when he measures up their education,
it's natural a Scot should have in mind
his children should be taught their own tradition,
however much he views it with suspicion.

70

And I got tired of acting like a Janus,
gazing ahead while glancing to the rear,
a posture that perhaps I should explain thus:
ambition is to TV men a spear
which, stuck in from behind, is sure to pain us,
however much it makes us persevere.
To Scotland I returned a conservationist
to stem the loss of buildings that the nation missed.

71

To build a city Androcles once planned,
and asked the Delphian oracle where to root it.
While frying fish his soldiers had just panned
a grass fire started. When he tried to put it
out, a wild boar rushed for open land.
The King obeyed instructions. In pursuit it
was slain; Ephesus drawn up, nobly done;
town planning as a discipline begun.

72

Wearing more 'hats' than one confuses good folk
(no wonder if bare-headed you keep walking!)
on whom stern duty puts an early rude yoke
that leaves them little room for idle gawking,
whatever doubt some deep instinctual mood spoke.
To multi-coloured Fairbairn I was talking.
Do more than one thing, and they underrate you.
Do just one thing, he answered, *and they'll hate you.*

73

No, not exaggeration: I'm not sneering.
Like animals, our fears are quick to start.
Rub the veneer of speech, you'll find us baring
our claws and teeth, eyes savagely alert;
nations like individuals compeering.
Self-interest commands the leading part
and dominates the nature of our play,
whatever we, or politicians, say.

74

But solaces like poetry and wine,
a loving wife and happy family,
make us to quick forgetfulness incline;
while music lends familiarity
with the rich world of feeling and design
that shapes and keeps its own finality;
such are the only substances we're given
to fill the framework of imagined heaven.

75

I've had my share of poets, known a handful—
Norman MacCaig, Mackay Brown, Crichton Smith—
a friend each with his own poetic brand full
of what makes up a sense of place; the pith
of ancient contrasts such as keeps our land full
of differences, kin without the kith:
a land where Viking, Lowlander and Gael
are unified by name, to no avail.

76

Yet sense of place is nothing, lacking man.
The wilderness would bore beyond belief
were it not measured up within the span
of cultivation's narrowing relief,
reminding us though we both need and can
escape from others briefly, held in fief
of such intelligence as we possess
it's we who clothe the world in meaning's dress.

77

But there's a quality I'm always careful
of humanising since our basset-hound,
an expert starer-up at you, eyes prayerful,
the laureate of basset-nature found
in Edwin Morgan. Meaning by the lairful
from foreign poets' language he unbound;
wit and compassion matched in like ability,
the voice of an uncommon versatility.

78

I've taken tea with Eliot; with MacNeice
gone drinking, puzzled why his Celtic gloom
and hectic laughter never seemed to piece
together; heard Day Lewis fill a room
with spoken music, lending verse a lease
of life its silent merits don't assume;
talked music and had lunch with E M Forster
at Edinburgh and (oh yes!) in Gloucester.

79

I saw in London fragile Richard Strauss,
the last great master who could shake the heart
with ecstasy, before a cheering house
acknowledge its applause, turn and depart,
leaving our sad and bitter times to douse
that finished beauty for the stringent art
of Shostakovitch, irony and power
in music that outlived a tyrant's hour.

80

For him, like Strauss, it was the world's ear
that listened, then the ear of time itself,
reflecting the anxiety and fear
that keeps afloat our age of measured wealth,
where semi-cloistered Britten let us hear
his half of life. On many a college shelf
dust gathers on the scores of played-once prizes
while silence wipes out aleatoric noises.

81

Francis George Scott, compared with Strauss no master
(what stanza could contain Scott's boisterous roaring!)
and yet of Scottish song a gifted caster,
into a few his Border genius pouring;
a music Scotland had allowed flow past her
soundless since Knox began his graceless goring:
Scott of the chiselled head, poetic teacher
lacking ambition's prop, an under-reacher.

82

Fine painters, too, I've numbered with my friends:
Anne Redpath, swirling poet of soft tones;
MacTaggart, whose romantic landscape blends
the sadness of spent evenings with lost dawns;
and Philipson, whose darting knife portends
the church's empty grandeur and the throne's,
strings fighting cocks with muscle, meditates
the shapes of love, the shadow of its hates.

83

Alas! the fate of most art is to stay put
where it began, and soon be quite forgotten.
But come to that, few people can uproot
themselves to move from where they were begotten;
when travel's cheap, their poverty's acute,
or some dictator simply says: *It's not on.*
So I've been lucky, able to enjoy
much travel. It's the little things annoy.

84

For instance, go to Italy or Spain
in the high season with a mob of British;
so constantly and rudely they'll complain,
your patience and your teeth will soon be grit-ish;
you'll wonder why they pay to buy such pain.
The life-and-soul-of-party ones grow skittish;
others want fish-and-chips and English telly,
declaring foreign drains are always smelly.

85

I like to travel with my wife alone
and let myself absorb the atmosphere;
those sights and sounds and scents together grown
that make an ancient place uniquely *here*;
what neither time nor wars have overthrown,
I like to view the gracious and the rare,
and celebrate in thankful meditation
such triumphs over much abomination.

86

It's not that I abhor my fellow men—
I loathe the stuck-up and the hoity-toity—
but long before a poet lifts his pen
his pregnant muse must keep her own society.
It's only through what swims into his ken
a writing man can add his little moiety
to that great store of what we all inherit,
from which we take more than we give, or merit.

87

Now that the world's afflictions reach us nightly
inside our homes, our minds erect protection
against such constant horror, brushing lightly
past conscience. Those who, by their own election,
devote their days to charity, and brightly
attempt to make some limited correction
find that like waves the poor come on; too many
not bettered by the billionth of a penny.

88

My wife in Turkey, eating shiskebab,
was stared at by a mangy prowling cat.
She threw it a small scrap. With a lean grab
it gulped it down. At once, from nowhere, pat
on cue, more cats appeared, each one a dab
at woeful staring, till a dozen sat
around her, ownerless and underfed.
For starving Turkish catdom her heart bled.

89

What's to be done? Keep down the population
of Turkish cats, or change the Turkish nature?
Or cultivate a sensitive frustration
that Asiatic cats must face a fate your
best friend would not wish on his worst relation?
Or, like some dotty Englishwoman, sate your
distress by feeding cats in countless numbers;
so that, though millions starve, your conscience slumbers?

90

Guiltily I admire the dedication
of those who use their strength against the leak
of bursting life that's born to face starvation,
its fate a listless year or two to eke
existence scratched from penny-pinched donation,
of which the gods of ignorance never speak.
But like all else, denial's a vocation
that finds its bleak reward, self-contemplation.

91

I'm conscious of the useless contribution
a symphony, a poem or picture makes;
but mankind's ache of ills wears no solution;
one trouble cured, and out another breaks.
Not even wisdom patiently Confucian
can feed the starving, heal the blood that cakes
on innocence, the always-losing side
in lying wars by dogma deified.

92

But numbers never multiply intensity;
a single victim knows the most of pain.
Though sprawling millions suffer, the immensity
is that one pattern over and again.
Our joy and sorrow's limited in density
it can't exceed, however much we'd fain
carry a broader burden. Thus denied,
the Christian myth needs Jesus crucified.

93

So art's the one resource an individual
can use to purify that sense of guilt
round each and every one of us decidual,
yet not be lured into the fatal silt
of shining superstitions, the residual—
so thinly spread, so generously spilt—
of status-seeking cruelties and lusts
religions use to prop their painted crusts.

94

Enough of that! It's through their own abstractions
the Scots get bogged and sink what's plain lucidity
with metaphysics' substitute for actions,
a devious disguise for hard cupidity.
I've had no time for party, clique or faction;
my constant search has always been for quiddity.
When properly grown tired of studying Man,
not God but earth, the healer's, what I scan.

95

My richest years were spent in Gartocharn;
Loch Lomond jagging distance blue with hills
endlessly ripping clouds that winds re-darn,
and gathering burns from winter's former chills.
Down battered rock and brackened ridge they churn,
hanging a silence white on distant rills,
shouldering thickened valleys far below,
their journey's breathing born of frozen snow.

96

The River Endrick, by whose whorling bank
we picnicked, sunned and sported summer days,
relaxed, gave up its surging pools and shrank,
a glitter threading fields of yellow haze
where, as we swam or splashed some children's prank.
we'd feel the flick of passing salmon graze
ankle or leg, our sense of apprehension
the mountained surface of the water's tension.

97

Riding the moorland, cantering the strand,
or fording, horses breast-high, streams and rivers,
we were a lazy motley-mounted band,
not dressed to kill, like hunting's easy-livers;
as happy fronting rain as in the bland
warmth of the sun, or moving through the shivers
of mountain valleys, silently alarming,
where summer's greening truce brings no disarming.

98

New neighbours born of ballads in the Borders,
grew passionate about their rolling acres,
where still they grouped inside their feudal orders.
Of tally-ho-ing we were not partakers,
of breeding bloodstock, never near afforders,
of riding, dear and formal, thus forsakers,
preferring over Annan's banks to roam,
its waters flowing past our Georgian home.

99

Three years I spent in Cumbria; Head's Nook
a shipping tycoon chose for his retreat,
leaving a village sounding like a joke
first built to serve his neo-Gothic seat.
We lived above a wooden glen. A brook
rehearsed beneath our windows its conceit
shrugged from the distant Pennines, whose cold range
gives England's east and west their interchange.

100

A terraced house in Greek Victorian style
brought our return to Glasgow, where the pace
of life had slackened; pile on crumbling pile
of tenements that once had housed a race
of purpose change had failed to reconcile,
bulldozed and cleared to leave uneven space;
its empty-handed workers gone, or slunk
into their own despair, its purpose shrunk.

101

All of us love the place of our nativity,
an instinct that we share with eels and salmon;
whether by wars or crime locked in captivity
or merely kept abroad through serving Mammon,
in youth's broad plains or age's steep declivity
the one affection that we rarely sham on.
Glasgow, it makes me sad to see how tumbled
your worldly image is, your influence crumbled!

102

For you have streets and terraces as splendid
as anything that Europe could produce
and—better late than never—you've expended
much conservation effort to induce
your golden stone to gleam as first intended.
Although it makes some Edinburgers puce
to hear it, your Victorian effulgence
no longer needs their Georgian indulgence.

103

What's gone for ever is the racing surge
of Glasgow feeling. It survived the slums,
a blunt alertness, its own end and urge,
reeking togetherness like clarty lums.
It's swept away with deprivation's scourge,
not showing up on screened computers' sums.
To say such things makes planners grow dyspeptic;
at least their Glasgow's much more antiseptic.

104

In cities, as in states, affairs of gravity
too often leave poor commonsense in tatters,
the public weal abandoned in some cavity
exposed when party dogma's all that matters.
Then, no amount of politicians' suavity
can heal the damage prejudice thus shatters:
we vote down leaders, raise the opposition
to find we haven't varied our condition.

105

However much we rage at the confusion
that clogs our wheeled economy, the fact is
the dream of faultless order's an illusion.
At least the muddled freedom we enact is
more pleasant than dictatorship's obtrusion,
when individuals find the social pact is:
Believe just what you're told, or be suppressed;
the State's the ultimate good; the State knows best.

106

How easily such generalities
blow up when near to politics we're veering!
It's only those who practise caring qualities
achieved by piecemeal social engineering,
and use the hard-won vague formalities
democracy depends on, should be steering
the ship of state; that leaky, lumbering boat
that, come what may, must keep us all afloat.

107

Though frail democracy has never ceased
breathing its message to whatever tongue
the rights of human liberty are leased,
there's no belief that flaunted time's not flung
to fragments, its accepted spells released
for scholars of dry death to nose among,
and marvel how credulity held charms
to shield against mortality's alarms.

108

Beware of him applauded on a rostrum
naïve with self-conceit that fortifies,
who claims he's found the one sure-curing nostrum,
fanaticism voltaging his eyes.
His remedy must prove a postulatum
of worn-out dogma decked in weak surmise.
It doesn't matter whose the hand that shoots:
you're dead. But life holds no such absolutes.

109

Having lived through the world's worst yet convulsion
and watched it heal the wounds and struggle towards
a kind of peace that holds its own compulsion,
nuclear horror checking savage hordes
who'd sweep through Europe but for this repulsion,
with anger I reject the traitorous words
of those who claim vast armies mean no harm,
for meek example bid the rest disarm.

110

In continents of envy, men not greatly
unlike ourselves sit planning our destruction,
forcing us match their weapons, hoping straightly
such tit-for-tat may prompt the sane deduction:
should either side attack, then desperately
both will go down through one atomic suction;
what man has fashioned through ten thousand years
annihilated; atavistic fears

111

that once he ranged pre-history with, prove stronger
than all he gained through his inquiring mind,
his reasoned, civilising values wrong; or
not sure enough to shape what they defined.
A sterile earth's swirled gases aeons longer
than luckless man's pathetic, glorious kind;
and could again revolve such timeless slack,
the human burden shaken off its back.

112

Those cushioned strategists who think that killings's
inevitable—quite a noble pastime—
charged up with threats and platitudes, seem willing
to kid themselves that life beyond the blast time
would still go on; that no atomic grilling
could ever truly prove a human last time.
Some might survive, to animals mutated:
it's peaceful life we want perpetuated.

113

Even now there's power deployed ten times too much
to still the world, kill everything that moved.
Whose finger might provide destruction's touch?
And if it did so, what would it have proved?
The fearful curse of human power is such
it digs itself a rut so deeply grooved
that source and purpose are alike forgot,
and all must be possessable—or nought!

114

Such scaring matters easily depress us;
might seem, perhaps, too serious for versing.
Not priests but poets sometimes best confess us,
give balance, sending warning-clouds dispersing.
There's Nature's here-and-now around to bless us,
discharging might-have-beens from needless nursing,
reminding us we aren't too meticulous
thinking self-frightened death a whit ridiculous.

115

To give much thought to might-have-beens is folly,
yet sometimes I regret my stubborn knees
could never make of Christmas more than holly,
the celebration when we try to please,
the time that shops relieve us of our lolly
as conscience gets no cheaper to appease.
How comfortable thinking you're aware of
a faith that means *Forever's* taken care of!

116

The more so since on hills that claim St Patrick
(though doubtless he was born on Irish soil)
I live, a superstition-cured agnostic
(St Peter, you can put that on your file!)
creature of Europe's culture, mainly Catholic,
its flower, delight, though nurtured in old guile.
Which goes to prove that pleasures rarely come
without some shadowed pain's residuum.

117

I look across the silver-threaded Clyde,
its summer banks a gleam of banding copper
doused grey beneath each spilling of the tide.
The water flecks and flees, a running chopper
abrupt with winter into which a slide
of mountain thick with storm can't put a stopper;
trees creak; the whole house whistles disarray.
Our guests admire the view, though, either way.

118

Here, in old age, I mock pontificators
in titled jobs of which they're briefly holders,
secured by Commons privilege or gaiters,
who, warning us of pebbles, trip on boulders;
Trade Union bullies, marching nuclear praters
(a clutch of waiting antis in their folders)
while millions suffer since the words most needed
are nowhere said; or, hinted at, unheeded.

119

In poetry, warned Shelley, don't embody
of right and wrong your own time-bound conception;
(although to some it seems a trifle odd he
so frequently allowed himself exception).
It is, indeed, a self-inflicted rod, the
too frequent use of which meets rough reception
from those who love to show off in a naughty pose,
yet think poetic moralising otiose.

120

Much verse I've written of the kind called heavy,
but now, however shrill the critics rage—
MacIncomplete, Courageous and the bevy
round Grecian Glen, or Portobello's sage—
I've done with paying up ambition's levy,
am quite without desire to be a mage;
so laugh where once I wept, and choose to write
a kind of verse indubitably light.

121

Auden proclaimed no poem he had written
had saved a single Jew from being gassed.
If he had hoped to do so, then he'd bitten
off more than art can chew, and was surpassed
by the great Christian God who chose to sit on
his silence while by thousands Jews were massed,
allowing man to exercise free will
doing the things he's best at: starve and kill.

122

They'd disagree who think the world is running
to some celestial plan, and so has meaning,
a viewpoint I've no difficulty shunning.
I can't believe in fate whose ravelled skeining
is changed by trivial chance and mindless gunning.
The earth, I think's, an accident, careening
through time and space whose stuff we can't conceive,
indifferent to everything we cleave.

123

Those stars that mariners thought everlasting
splutter to cinders through the dark they lace;
the silver moon has no more spells for casting
since astronauts have bounced upon her face;
the cloth of heaven, its white-robed saints repasting
while angels harp, lies crumpled in disgrace:
Eternity's not there for our alighting;
it's cosmic junk that rocket probes are sighting.

124

To find ourselves, however accidental,
alive, enjoying children, Mozart, wine,
such countless pleasures, bodily and mental,
as we are given to pass along the line
here in a world to which we owe no rental,
one sexing link in nature's close design,
is wonderful enough without obtaining
a *why* and *wherefore* which there's no explaining.

125

Through grandchildren we see our hopes projected
just when we feel that soon we'll be disbanded;
their mix of genes, by chance and love selected,
two pasts reshuffled, dealing single-handed
whatever cards heredity's elected
(though fortunately can't yet be commanded)
to play another spanning of the game
of human life with, never twice the same.

126

Ahead, there's darkness. Death comes as the end.
Of this we have as little right complaining
as not possessing centuries to spend,
or lining up to watch Rome's legions training
or having Willie Shakespeare for a friend.
The universe in all its wide sustaining
will fall, they say, into a final black hole,
succeeded then by nothingness's slack whole.

127

As years pile up their tiny little load, a
man feels his strength and faculties declining.
Since I'll not be around to write a coda
(dear reader, don't pretend that you're repining!)
I'll pour myself a whisky dashed with soda
and draw one last conclusive underlining—
Farewell, my muse! For you, my darling wife,
and everything you gave us, thank you, life!

VII

Poems from *A Net to Catch the Winds* (1981),
The French Mosquitoe's Woman (1985),
Requiem for a Sexual Athlete, Glasgow (1989),
Scotland: An Anthology (1989), *Uncollected* (1989–90)

A Celebration
(for Joyce, on our forty-fifth wedding anniversary)

Brightly sunlight flecked upon
that delightful seaside lawn
where my love first stirred; where you,
young in beauty, let me woo;
woo and win you, take away
what transforms our human clay;
sustenancing love that blends
in creation, and so lends
humans what a god might know
shaping ages long ago
through the fantasies of Man
long before his mind outran
mazed religions, dogma's laws,
homing on the uncaused cause,
when burst atom or black hole
swallowed up the ghostly soul.

Wonder is the only fee
lovers still have left to pay
for the flesh's trembling share
of the future it must bear;
for its children's reaching grasp
to undo the hidden hasp
on the gate of the unknown
time itself has not been shown;
gratitude the change returned
after all our passion's burned;
weathered flesh a tale well told
leaving memory to hold
hands, no longer nightly sent
caressing, quietly content.

Now, in evening hues that glow
over forty years ago
no pretentious hymn of praise
to a mythic God I raise
out beyond the breadths of space
plunging rockets can't outpace;
but within one mortal span
praise the only way I can.

167

For the mysteries we paired;
for the happiness we bared;
for the you that made of me
more than I could ever be
in experience alone;
for the seasons we've outgrown;
for the oneness that you bring,
by your presence substancing
what would otherwise seem mere
outline, wanting comfort's cheer;
for all these and more besides
daily as the certain tides,
my total's sum, my parcel's part,
thanks with all my ancient heart.

An Inverness Hotel

Outside the restless window of my sleep
seagulls rip aside the dawn's caul.
I stagger through to life, pull back the curtains
and watch them scissoring the mottled scraps
of yesterday's discarded human refuse
that waits for shuffling binmen to remove.

Snap-hunting amateur photographers
fall for them every time; puffily folded,
winking on rusty bollards; in the wake
of churning ships, quick dips of wing, long glides
that boast them masters of their element;
or dropping streaks, white as themselves, on decks,
abandoned quays or fresh-ploughed coastal fields.

It is, perhaps, their dazzling isolation
that fascinates us, smooth in company;
the rocks they breed on inaccessible,
the death they die an unaccountable plunge
seawards; lonely and final as a plane,
into whose jets they sometimes blunder, tumbles,
a vanished blob gone off a radar screen
that signals for a while our brief concern.

Seagulls leave no trace of their own wreckage.

In Orkney

A headless carcase slumped on a butcher's shoulder
from lorry to shop in a city's hungry street
sent me in mind to Orkney, years ago;
a dappled field of cows and a schoolboy dare.
Lie down, they said: let the creature lick your face.

I lay sweet in that young grassy place:
the cows advanced, each through its own stare.
Their tongues roughly caressed my skin with a slow
assurance, till I leapt to my winner's feet,
their animal shadows lengthened; older, colder.

Spokesperson's Apology

If we don't sell them stuff, then others will,
since self-defence has rights that none can shun,
and Britain must put money in her till.

Boys will be boys. Arms aren't sold to kill,
for Peace stares out the muzzle of a gun.
If we don't sell them stuff, then others will.

Who'd vote more tax to foot the nation's bill?
From such a notion politicians run;
yet Britain must put money in her till.

Flesh blasts apart, or cooks, a napalm grill;
most cools in bed, its thread of life unspun.
If we don't sell them stuff, then others will.

What does it matter how you round the hill
since priests affirm that Death has been undone,
and Britain must put money in her till?

There's no escape through logic's wordy skill:
fighting's the show with quite the longest run.
If we don't sell them stuff, then others will,
and Britain must put money in her till.

Peter Pan

Do you believe in fairies?, the eternal boy asks
as a waving spotlight fingers the darkened stage.
If so, applaud. Self-consciously, we applaud.
A joke, of course. Mere children's make-believe;
for who would hold back time to disengage
the failures knowing secretly forbodes?

Good, good! Then Tinkerbell is saved,
a wish that all experience corrodes.
The children laugh as public adult masks
relax for them, and eagerly clutch the sleeve
of one, at least, secure; their household god;
not knowing who he thought it was had waved.

Scotland the What?

Six men out of seven who applied to us for executive jobs withdrew their
application when they learned that the job was in Scotland.

*Report by a firm of Management Consultants, quoted
in 'The Glasgow Herald'*

Scotland's image? You must be joking!
The less said about that, the better.
Bagpipes and haggis; tourist-broking
half-rainbow framed. A dead letter
dropped out of Europe's circulation.
Rounds of soliciting applause
for each enticed investing nation.
Ragbag of pound notes, ancient laws
and sour religion. Land whose thrust
once fashioned factories and ships
that shaped a reputation's trust.
A past that's locked by tightened lips
relaxing sentimental farce.
History's biggest little thinkers;
adjusting deferential blinkers
where politics and patronage speak
louder than risk or principle.

Quick takers-on of petty pique
reason proves unconvincible.
Proud worshippers of the dull and thick
confusing numbers with perception.
Romanticists whose ultimate trick
is swallowing their self-deception.
Scotland's image? The hell with it!
I love; I hate; I curse; I care
that we should let ourselves submit
might be to *what we think we were.*

Retiring

A leathery old poet, sixty-five,
fashions this sonnet out of gratitude
that here, to be demobilised, he should
with mind and muse and body whole arrive;
his shaping words still able to contrive,
and hold secure against vicissitude
of memory or temperature of mood,
the little of what's past that stays alive.
Of life's quick touch and go he's had his share:
youth and the naked compass of its charms;
music that comforts comfortless despair;
ambition, hung with struggles and alarms;
the relics of what's left all he can wear
till death's commanding nothingness disarms.

Grandchild Visiting
(for Carrie Leigh Barr)

She stands, her chubby knees gently swaying,
before the shapes on the television screen,
unaware of the hate the words are spraying,
or what the murdered falling bodies mean.

Through his own screams a baddie bites the floor.
The colours cease to hold her. *Look, here's me,*
the nosing basset saunters through the door;
and, innocent with love, she cries: 'Toe-*bee*'!

On Trial

I THE PRISONER

She stumbled from the cells into the dock,
constables corsetting her, and roundly glared
at the swivel faces; each, she imagined, paired,
few of them having found their flesh's lock
picked and sprung by a friend; the sudden shock
of warmth withdrawn, the emptied things once shared
spat at by tender words flung back to mock.

But the evidence closed her in; how, high on fury,
she'd threatened the tender throats of the little boys
he'd gotten on her; as the picture built, she
recalled the discovering neighbours, folk like the jury;
the resistant knife, the gashed unnatural noise,
and, then as now, the eyes that chorused Guilty.

II BUSINESS MAN

Firmed by the strictures of self-rectitude
that years of work and marriage couldn't bend,
and having checked his standards that it could
in no way pious principles offend,
clearing his throat, why yes, he said, he'd lend
his long consideration to becoming
the Jury Foreman. He would comprehend
disordered facts the others might find numbing.
Authority then set his fingers drumming
impatiently with those who faltered doubt,
despite his easy clarity of summing
up statements rung with truth and those without:
pity was weakness that he couldn't own
while compromise was failure, weakly shown.

III SOCIOLOGIST

He flopped the inequalities of the world
on a hard seat, let attentiveness unfold
and, though he felt as if his spine had curled,
heard the snap of a tether lose the hold
it briefly strained on the flawed reality
of a system proffering only its crust to the poor,
keeping the softer posture of society
for those advantage rendered worth the lure.

Guilt and conviction simply didn't arise
when the weakness of manipulated shame
let a sociologist widely visualise
what shaped the contours that are miscalled blame.
Did she or not?, the impatient foreman rasped;
drowning in straws, *she did*, the false one gasped.

IV POP SINGER

He must have been down on the uppers of his luck
to touch that broad, the pop musician mused
on the small screen of his mind as it reviewed
the groping hand, the skirt pushed into a ruck,
the struggle with pants, then the quick loveless fuck.
How otherwise could a guy be so little cued
as to marry the bitch and beget a battering feud
that left her big with a second and him stuck?

You'd think from then on he'd have had no truck
with women; yet he'd got his pecker glued
to the next available ass that needed screwed,
or offered herself in the street for an easy buck:
Guilty or not?, he heard the foreman say,
rousing the answer: *Eh?—oh, yeah, yeah!*

V SCHOOLTEACHER

A funny thing, thought the vagueing classical scholar
after the hours of evidence and the weight
of having to measure out the disposable fate
of a woman smudged away by grinding squalor—
Medea, Jeannie Goldsmith, whatever you call her
didn't matter—centuries couldn't abate
the risks the legs rode when the animal state
let naked lust bestride its reeking holler.

Without a wasted second, thankfully back
in the paper streets that argued Ancient Rome,
he surveyed his pupils, oddly never at home
in the past, and sighed at their present lack
of respect for certificates and the clean-limbed rule
that bested all the days of his life at school.

VI NOVELIST

Truth, grey prophets beard, is stranger than fiction!
As a novelist, I'm sure I'd never have got
away with such an unoriginal plot;
two people rubbing into open friction,
whatever they said implying contradiction,
the straight thing twisted into counterplot,
exasperation tindering the knot
that joyed them once in fleshing benediction.

Starved of his sex and lacking love's conviction,
with jewellery and drink he easily bought
the only element he'd ever sought,
leaving her oiling jealousy's affliction.
How odd our thoughtful glands secrete a mess
that oozes murder. *Then she did it? Yes.*

VII   CHARLADY

I wuz luikan fur a leak in the waashin machine,
the door wuz aff the sneck fur the watter tae rin
oot, whan all o a sudden I heard the quean
screich. An awfu commotion. It was kin
o eerie like, sae ah sez tae masel, I'll see gin
onythins wrang wi Jeannie. Whit wi her man
cairryan oan wi lassies he'll nivver see
again, her heidaches, an she sae deidpan
wi it all, ah thocht, ah'll gie her a cup o tea.
But whan ah opened her front door, losh me!
she was cooriean, cover't wi bluid on the haa stair,
a carvin knife in her haun, an baith the wee
laddies mangl't deid on the livin-room flair
Ah've kill't the bairns, she sabbed; *it makes nae sense . . .*
Nothing to ask, snapped Counsel for the Defence.

VIII   THE UNDECIDED

A face that burrowed a moustache to hide in
sat amongst those who never held strong views;
good people, always eager to confide in
others just how hard it was to choose,
preferring always movement with a crowd;
readers of tabloids tarting up the news
to titillating entertainment, loud
with scandals, murders, rapes and sexual stews.
All of which shook their heads to virtuous *tuts*,
yet proved essential reading for relaxing;
this was for real, a maze of *ifs* and *buts*,
the arguments, bewilderingly taxing;
a flock of fundamentalist Don't Knows,
Guilty, if you all say so, I suppose.

IX   THE QCs

There are pressures in life that cannot be withstood,
Defending Counsel proclaimed in defiant mood
to the dusty Gothic rafters; *however good*
we humans are, the pressures that obtrude
on reason can betray the normal heart
from such affections as it holds most dear.
Said Counsel for the Prosecution: *The part*
the defendant played on the fatal night is clear
beyond all possible doubt—She cut the throats
of her sons with full responsibility
for her actions. That's the matter's nub.
After the jury had cast its clumsy votes,
Pretty well cut and dried, said the old QC
to the younger, over sherry in the Club.

X   THE JUDGE

The voice which penetrated from the wig
that justice evened centuries with, pronounced
its final measured peroration, big
with public gravitas, before it pounced
upon the prisoner's forfeit liberty:
Crime passionel, peculiar to the French
and not the outcome of conspiracy,
in Scottish law affords no just defence.

Weeping, the broken woman disappeared;
reporters raced to hype her story up
to catch a morning's glance; the courtroom cleared;
the judge disrobed and wandered home to sup,
then take down Homer for the umpteenth time,
lost in the ancient lineage of crime.

Three Translations

I   GIFTS
(after the Chinese of Lao Tsu, c 500 BC)

Most parents wish, before their child is born,
A babe with high IQ, dear Lord, allot me.
I, who possessed it, hold the gift in scorn,
since precious little worldly gear it got me.
The baby, blunt as an unsharpened knife,
will never feel self-doubting's cuts, the sinister
unceasing edge that pares the tranquil life;
so could, in time, become a Cabinet Minister.

II   DRY BREAD
(from the German of Paul Heyse)

My appetite has gone, I'll eat no more,
for in my foot a painful thorn has stuck.
Though left and right I look, and both implore,
where lovers are concerned, I'm out of luck.
A little man would keep me quite contented
if he respected me, and just consented
to tell me of his love; a neat-made fellow,
a veteran like me, his views as mellow
as mine are. Put quite bluntly, what I mean
is some old chap who's aged about fourteen.

III   THE SONG
(after the Italian of Quasimodo)

I met a bland composer in the street.
Look, he said: *I've set one of your poems:*
I'll bring it to your flat and let you hear it.
I'm three floors up, I said: *I've no piano.*
He said: *Don't worry. I'll bring a piano with me.*
We'll get it up there somehow. Then you'll listen
detached, at ease, to what I've made your poem.
I said: *Don't bother. I should lose ten minutes:*
and who could ever get them back for me?

Programme Note
by Hausen Berenze, for the Instruction of His Musicians

My works's the symbiosis of the future,
Therefore the piece consists of an arc, stretching
precisely over two hours fifty seconds.
The arc arises out of an E and C
the orchestra reiterates in unison,
swinging from the top of the interval
to show that no arc holds finality.
This lasts for thirteen minutes fifteen seconds,
growing gradually to a climax.
Ten sections of the players then embellish
the interval in several different keys
chosen by cleaners and platform attendants.

The music rises to another climax.
Thirty minutes later, the third bassoon
gets to his feet and, through an amplifier,
declaims, with swelling volume, twenty times
in varied tones, O WORLD O LIFE O TIME.
At the mention of time, the musicians break its bondage,
and, for the next hour, aleatoric freedom
is given to each player. They react
as they see fit to what the words suggest.
Then, give or take a breath, the principal flautist
with his (or her) right index finger, presses
the starter button of the tape recorder.
The sounds I've plotted on a synthesiser
will dominate all else. Tubas and trumpets
leave their seats and, weaving through the players,
stand by the oboes. Wilfully they struggle
to drown the electronic oscillations.
They will, of course, succeed. The tape concludes
as suddenly as it begins. Thus, order
through freedom of expression is triumphant.
Loudly, the opening third, but now inverted,
C up to E (since every arc completed
implies the next begun) is once more sounded.

Cellists and oboeists change instruments
to signify the chaos of the wrap
of space around the order art imposes.
Then the conductor, who will have been sitting
at a locked organ consol (representing
the death of bourgeoise values) must get up
on the organ bench, and through a megaphone
roar out THE REST IS SILENCE. Timpanists
advance to the rostrum, holding up their sticks
then, legs akimbo, facing the audience,
beat silence on capitalistic air.
Precisely at two hours fifty seconds,
they turn and strike the leader with their left sticks.
Immediately my music ceases, finished
until the next time it is re-created.

I consider applause aristocratic decadence,
since liking or not liking is irrelevant
to the new music's purpose; and to mine.
So I wish indoctrinated Marxists, dressed
like shop stewards in plain clothes, at every row-end
to quell this vulgar habit of applause.
I, Hausen Berenze, give my music,
the future's open voice, to you my sisters
and brothers who with me believe that music,
like politics, should freely be enforced.
The notes are yours, the royalties are mine.

The Music Critic's Dream

Not so much scrappy signatures, the sound
of Berg and Webern, as the screen
on which were pitched the silences between,
outstretched my patience with the unprofound
*Stille an Diotima.** Not yet bound
to praise what's well approved but doesn't mean
much, and being a kind of music 'Green',
I laughed when they applauded. How they frowned!
An Inspector from the Department of Pseuds came round
next morning. *Look,* he said, *You haven't seen
this music's fundamental aniline—*
a pompous ass deserving to be downed.
It's to the heart that music must be true,
I cried: *so no to Nono—and to you!*

---

* A 'Fragmente for String Quintet' based on a poem by Hölderlin.

Nocturne

In the middle of the night, the footless hours,
my fears take courage, crowd about my bed.
Leaning over me, the false breath
of their alarm chokes me. I rehearse
    the gasp of my own death.

In the morning, in the blood's awakening,
whey-faced, they slink away. A sunned-out moon
circles my living's dark side. Man again,
I wonder what it is they want of me:
    Or rather, how, and when?

Two Odes

I *BRIEF ODE IN DISHONOUR OF MUZAK*

Whenever two or three are gathered together,
there you will be, as sightless as religion,
to soothe collective confidences, whether
with feeble, clichéd sequences, or pidgined
tunes of the great forced back upon themselves.

Repetitive as travellers through hotels
hoisted to floors in plushy elevators,
waiting to lose a tooth or find a cure
wherever planes or trains hold congregators,
beneath the supermarket's cut-price lure,
the squirting aerosoling muzak swells
killing the fear of which dead silence smells
to comfort those decisions leave unsure.

II *AN AUGUSTAN ODE TO ONE WHO URGED*
A RETURN TO VICTORIAN VALUES

Back to Victorian values? Was she poking
fun at us? Few fires conceal their smoking.

Let's imagine sitting on that fence
between command and meek subservience.

Hail! ceremonious land of hope and glory,
absorbing others in its story
against their weak unprofitable wills
whose destiny an Empire best fulfils.
See, British oceans floating raw material
conquered and plundered for the Crown Imperial
whose workshop of the world makes sellers rich
while beggars gutter crusts by lane or ditch;
where monied bosses crack a breaking pace,
the poor stay in their vast respectful place,
their ultimate experience, disgrace;
religion whinges, prettified and sweet,
though not to urchins in the ragged street;

the well-heeled condescending grace of charity
dresses herself to look like moral parity;
thinking of England, wifely legs outspread
with love a softening word no longer said
except to puffy prostitutes who throng
the piety that conscience learns to wrong;
such endless parturition, such a swelling
of tiny deaths for graveyard tombstone-telling;
the brashly vulgar songs; for some, the benison
of puzzling thoughts by Browning or Lord Tennyson;
piano legs and chairs draped out in lace;
nick-nacks and whatnots glazed behind a case;
the snobbish blood, the pampered empty minds
of tittle-tattlers bustling their behinds;
bare exploitation with a double face . . .

The perfect ideal for the human race?

Back to Victorian values! Was she joking,
or calculating headlines by provoking?
Or just another politician croaking
to jack-Poll figures up another place?

Fifty Years On: Variations On a Glasgow Theme

I   CHILDHOOD

From my bedroom window, over a riding sea
of slate-gray roofs, I watched the cranes on the Clyde
slowly shaking their uncertain heads. I relied
on them, mist or darkness, simply to be
there, ridgedly guarding what it meant
to belong to Glasgow: a warm feeling inside
when people spoke of craftsmanship; a pride
that generations long since gone had lent.
Then, on a summer paddle-steamer freighted
with happiness, I marvelled from the deck
as, under propped-up hulls where DEAD SLOW
was ordered by the river bank, a bated
wonder seized me. What storms were their's to trek
that we now passed as if on tip-toe?

II   I REMEMBERED SABBATHS

The bells clang to each other, street by street,
furthering distance, tossing clamour down
on the damp flagstone pavements of a town
emptied for Sunday. Cautiously discreet,
the dressed-up worshippers group in hushes; greet
like casual strangers, each as if on loan
so couldn't be the first to cast a stone
against such managed communal deceit.
O God, speak to our hearts that we may feel
forgiveness for our sins, the minister prays,
while clumsily these borrowed people kneel;
but only silence meets his tremulous brays;
so up they rise on knees of suppled zeal,
reclaim their sinful selves and take their ways.

III   ASSEMBLING

Ye gates, lift up your heads, we challenged our school
assemblies fifty resonant years ago,
though not one gloried angel deigned to show
who would be blown to bits, who'd drudge, who'd rule,
or who might find the technological tool
to ratchet forward what we think we know;
always a distance-dreamer, nobody's fool,
recording scribbler, I had less to show.
Meeting together, old age the common fix,
it wasn't trade winds taken that we talked;
or whoring fame that briefly shadow-stalked,
but who was capped for what in 'Thirty-six;
as if achievement, husk-like, fell away,
bragging us back to emptied yesterday.

IV DREAMS AND DESTINATIONS

Fixed in a family album, the eager boy
flattens the freckled envy of his nose
against a shop-front window, where a toy
train, retracing circles, stops and goes,
while signals flash blind sanction, carriages gleam
their tiny emptiness and figures wait
on platforms, posturing to make it seem
they left too early or arrived too late.
An old man greets those staring photographs,
so long away, across such varied ground,
still separated, as by glass that halves
the distance his ambition ran him round;
and, inside looking out now, quietly laughs
that somehow journeys' ends remain unfound.

V CURTAINS

Discarded curtains on a sale room floor,
velour, dark crimson, but the texture bare;
a dusty heap of cloth. Yet, as I stare,
I see them living, through a childhood door
I can't now enter; watch my mother pour
coffee for those around the fireside; hear
my father call for music, and an air
of Mozart's; feel my lost self ring the chore
of shutting darkness and the thickened roar
of traffic out; the inarticulate fear
of weighted menace somehow gathered there
that, should it break, must carry all before.
The wave has cast and carried; all are gone,
and thin the thread their memory hangs upon.

VI   THE FALL OF THE LEAF

Dry leaves rattle, scuttling down Great George Street
as frosted Autumn pinches the pallid air,
their pungency of breath the drift to where,
some fifty years ago, I'd wait to greet
a girl; talk nothings and arrange to meet
next day, and next; her springing frizzy hair,
half-hinted breasts and gently puzzled stare,
still distanced promise yearning to entreat.
Now, from the far side, stained with time's defeat,
I smell the leaves and watch another pair
press slimnesses together, unaware
how brief the fruited centre, or how sweet:
and cry my ghosts of passion, deaf as hell,
a shabby Faustus with no soul to sell.

VII   IN TUITION

A door-to-door seller of underwear
for ladies, Plymouth Brethren persuasion,
had a plain daughter; stern, with rusty hair,
who talked God into permanent liaison.
Stiffened by starch, straight Wilhelmina Baikie
attempted to arrest my falling curve
of mathematic prowess, always shaky;
though firm, she thought, beside the moral swerve
of poetry and music I adored—
pleasures that must be constantly repeated,
she feared, *unlike refreshment in the Lord;*
complacency, assuredly broad-seated,
admitting that we both had to relieve
the dailyness of life with make-believe.

VIII IN HER DAY

Dead at ninety-three, the last of her twenties kind,
she viewed the world as if it were an infection.
She'd lean from the ancient deeps of her stiff-backed Rolls, and
   wind
the window down to wrinkle her nose at the choice selection
of nectarines and peaches brought out to her from Russells,
the florist and fruiterer. While prodding her objection,
the earthy things—potatoes, turnips, Brussels—
were packed obsequiously for chauffeur collection.
Even the faded house, where those of good connection
were hushed inside by a stately parlourmaid,
in getting sold for flatting was guilty of disaffection
to the memory of one who'd kept such standards, it was said,
that before she'd give consent to her final removal,
had Death brought in to suffer her approval.

IX THE VIOLIN MAKER

The other day, the first in fifty years,
I passed the faded shop of Andrew Smillie
where I, a shadow boy, stood watching while he
planed violins, or plied with soft veneers
from pots of sunshine, old and darkly embered,
the delicate white shapes, so like a woman's;
caressed the new-born sound, so like a human's,
the dearth of all our yesterdays remembered.
He'd have me listen while a group of friends
blended four lines of notes upon a page
that Haydn ordered in a courtly age;
from questing means, unanswerable ends.
It's now a depot freeing dust from Hoovers:
time must have its residue-removers.

X   LEAVING INNELLAN, SEPTEMBER 1939

Fifty years on, I remember leaving behind
my boyhood world of broadcast threats, outgrowing
the privileges common to my kind,
the sliding years there was no means of slowing
gone with the lingered hours I spent reclined
upon a lawn I'd used the peace up mowing:
war, to whom we'd secretly assigned
our youth, our future, claimed what we were owing.
Soon to be sweeping seas hostilities mined,
a paddle-steamer took me, no light showing,
across a twilight Firth whose clouds defined
the lost regrets of yesterday's unknowing.
Fifty years on, like fifty million dead—
statistics, meaningless as soon as said.

XI   THE NECROPOLIS

Christ, they believed, reserved their heavenly mansion,
so they built its lodge on Glasgow's Necropolis hill,
the makers and breakers who clashed with iron will:
men for whom life meant double, triple expansion,
who, assured in death, still felt obliged to fill
an expected position, aloof in proud seclusion;
have architects raise turrets of illusion
on templed pinnacles against earth's chill.
Over their scuttled threshold rats pass,
a tramp shelters his hours of empty hurting,
two furtive lovers slope, illicitly skirting:
alas, the grey light sighs to sodden grass.
All that lies here oblivion has misted,
only the charnel-houses being listed.

XII   BBC MAN IN ST ANDREWS

Young man, the Professor of Anatomy said;
no one will ever walk upon the moon
till long years after you and I are dead.
Philosophers might ask, How soon is soon?
Before his judgement crumbled to the grave
or I had used up half life's afternoon,
ballooning men, laconically brave,
like soft-foot children on a trampoline,
bounced on the orb that over centuries gave
imaging poets their celestial sheen;
brought back chipped sterile rock, a handful of dust,
and calculations of what it could mean
for us who, on our tiny cooling crust,
go fabricating gods to lend us trust.

XIII   THE GIRL FROM NEWTON MEARNS

O Lord, since Thou omnipotently knowest
all that occurs within Thy servant's heart;
and since whatever things are there, Thou sowest,
of blame Thou'llt surely take a little part.
Last Wednesday, as down the street I goest,
I saw a woman looking much more smart
yet wearing just the same as me. Ah woest!
Pretending but to stumble, with a smart
kick from my heel, she, falling, overthrowest
a vendor's fruit and vegetable cart.
The man without Thy sense of quid pro quoest,
then called me, Lord, a careless fuckan tart!
Forgive me, Lord, though he was not the beauest . . .
somehow I had to pay Thy debt I owest.

XIV INT IT?

Jings! The lites are gaun up in George Square;
an weez jist three weeks hame frae the Coasta Brava,
whaur yous that waants the flamean sun can hava
bo-nanza. It wuznae jist sic a rare tare
fur Jimmy an me. Weez waantit a Spanish bint.
Aa richt wigglan their bums an noakin pie-ella,
but try tae git aff wi wan an . . . senyor! . . . they smella
rat if yur no a creeshy dago. Shame, int
it? An Xmas oanly ninety shoapan days . . .
fur them wi the dirt! . . . och, isnae yon fantaastic!
Bulbs oan the blink an fairy-tales in plastic!
Jist think. If they hadnae goat Jesus born, ah sez,
thaed nivveruv goat the hail thing oaperational:
nae crucifixion! Sez Jimmy: *Yur sensational!*

XV UNEMPLOYED

Ah clipt an dyed ma heid tae luik lik a burd.
Sumkina coakatwo ur mebbe a parrat.
ma faither sez. The auld fule's bluidy absurd!
Whoiver saw thae things in punk an carrat?
Fur the likes of weez yins wi no the smell o a joab—
the effan burroo an the lass's nippy sodderan—
whaurs thur tae turn ti bit yur frienly moab
thae saxty gloryus years till wur duin an dodderan?
Bit jeez, they noatice. They canna forget wur here
whan we hugger the streets ur stoap at the Central Stacshun.
Pretendan no tae geck, yi can feel thur fear
wur sumthun yi catch, lik the cauld ur constipaeshun.
Weel, sniff yur toaffy noses; jist sniff them full;
it's easier faan doun than gaen up a hull!

XVI   AN INCIDENT

It wuznae until ahd had the chance o a real guid blether
that ah heard the hail story frae her across the landin.
Efter ahd pusht the bride's chimean door-bell, standan
there wuz the polis. Yi culduv felled me wi a feather.
The waddin pair wuz jist hame frae the registry,
toestan themsels an thur friens, a cupla drams an a sang,
when upstair knoackt his stick on the flair. Then the bell rang.
Him complainan aboot the noise. Ach, oan yir way—
it's no every day thurs a waddin, sez Jeannie, giean a shuv.
The door clattert the auld yin. He fell oan his bald heid
richt doun the stairs, where he lay pretendan tae be deid.
Sez I, ah sez: Wiv came wi the pairty's cairry-oot, guv.
Sez the polis: Thurull be nae pairty, sae cut oot the razz-ma-tazz.
Sez I: Yud think therud been a bluddy murder. Sez he: Thur has.

XVII   LONDON SCOTS

They've turned decaying warehouses into flats,
peopled again the office-emptied City;
won arguments with the new aristocrats
of profit, whose developed nitty-gritty
grinds out the more or less available cash;
wine-bars instead of tearooms; haute cuisine
replacing fish and chips or mince and mash;
the appetite for Glasgow, heritage-keen.
It isn't for real; it's done on yuppie money
much better spent on helping the unemployed
(to what?), streetwise, they grumble. To me, it's funny,
phoenixing leaves the wingless ones annoyed;
exiles especially when they famously say
Glasgow was friendlier slum-years away.

XVIII   SATURDAY AFTERNOON, ARGYLE STREET

The pavement shoves and pushes as the crowd,
intent on buying radios, cookers, shoes,
whatever claims a bargain, hears the loud
contending hucksters. *C'moan hen, whit's ti lose?*
Yuh'll no find pers ur peaches guid as these
fur twice the price. Yon's value, shrills a slouched
elided sound as crunkled money's changed
and, bagged by dirty hands, the fruit's debouched,
the deal complete, the buyer re-estranged.
But bargains shrink within the buyer's hand;
what's missing from the parcel is the patter,
those jokes that make supply create demand
and yet were somehow substance of the matter—
brash promises for sale that, once alone,
unwrapped, we find were more than what we own.

XIX   DEFINING CULTURE

In war-awaiting Glasgow, shoes were square-toed,
confrontational, closer to the bar,
plus foured, square-jawed, only aware they owed
a golfing handicap, on course for par;
culture was cars and cocktails, afternoon bridge,
thè dansants, plummy tennis, big-band jazz;
whether you owned a radiogram and a fridge,
were part of the with-it South-Side razzamatazz.
Today, it's Community Drama, the tabloid press,
what mindless football swears at, by, or does;
the telly, women's lib, sneering at 'cless,'
illiteracy taught to hate the 'fuzz.'
One kind of bleakness looks much like another.
If that's what Glasgow culture's about, why bother?

XX   GRANDFATHER AT THE CIRCUS

The smell of greasepaint, the outrageous band
oompahing with expectancy as clowns
bounce trouser-flopping jokes before the gowns
of acrobats are sloughed and, foot by hand,
they swing a sea of faces, worried frowns
lest he should slip or she mishear commands;
then elephants upened on their stands
succeed a trotting sheen of dappled browns.
Exciting shifts of colour if you're four,
too young to know the glister from the gold;
but long before you're many times as old,
beneath some heated crowd's expectant roar
you'll learn what's not for show and can't be told;
the sawdust scent of carnage and the cold.

XXI   ABOARD THE PADDLE-STEAMER 'WAVERLEY'

The last sea-going paddle-steamer in the world
phut-phutted through the Kyles of Long-ago,
aboard her still a ghost with hopes unfurled
when first she took the estuary, the slow
erosion of his possibilities
not yet withdrawn to haunt him, the no-go
areas of effort-proved futilities
not yet unmemoried nothings, left to show.

Indifferent to stratagems and checks
hills blue with shade glide monumentally past,
the next day's masters tigging on the decks
round one aware there's nothing to make fast
to, forced forever play catch-as-catch-can.
It seems only yesterday, sighed yesterday's man.

XXII   HARD OF HEARING

All that he lost at first were bits of chat—
Maisie's daughter five months pregnant; whether
she'd marry him; what Wullie might be at
if he wasnae sae bone idle; how a feather
fashioned new wonders from a faded hat;
the usual disappointment with the weather;
was secret drinking making Minnie fat?—
he'd nod agreement, needing no such blether.
But skies clotted silence; distance lent
further away; he found he strained to hear
soft music; splashy kindly people bent
much useless information to his ear.
Distorted from the inside, looking out,
All right!, he'd bellow. *There's no need to shout!*

XXIII   THIRTY-TWO ATHOLE GARDENS, W2

When I was a boy, stickily in my 'teens,
I thought there were feelings needing words to express
them, fix to their own memory; some means
to fetch conclusions out of the reach of guess;
sign off a sure *what happened in the end*;
settle a debt of doubt its final *yes*,
outlasting fashion's mirror-haunting trend
that leaves its own immediacy less.
Now, in Spring, when the chestnut's candelabra
flare pink flame, as they clustered years ago,
and sex has long since used up its abracadabra,
what flowers of certainty are there to show?
Doubts, freshly cracked, weed open veins of verse,
where I'm the last conclusion I rehearse.

XXIV   PLEASE DO NOT THROW AWAY YOUR TICKET

Everyone needs a storyline to hold
to, pitching untogether waves of facts;
life, less of what we see than what we're told,
not having been where accidents or acts
diverted history's course or cooled the mould
that shapes believing legends, then exacts
obedience to the fiction currently sold—
not guaranteed against what truth subtracts.
Encircled gaseous planets, flaming stone,
unbounded swarming millioned miles of space,
with only man-made stories to atone
the trust that animates our sense of place.
It doesn't matter if the tale's not true:
discard the fable, and what's left of you?

XXV   GEORGE SQUARE

Watching the hunger marchers fill George Square,
God! what a cock-up father's generation
has made of things, my callow indignation
would flash and, stiff with idealism, swear
we'd make a better showing; all to share
the goodies; each to fit his occupation;
fulfilment reached, the rounded destination:
somehow, we'd argue peace out of the air.
Fifty years later, hearing shouts and screams
protest their incoherence—cold and gone
my idealism—violence the themes
despair provides to variate upon,
for you, my father's ghost beyond extremes,
and for myself, I murmur: *Pardon, pardon.*

Impromptus

I   THE POETRY READING

When you write about Glasgow you only seem to see
the bad things razor-slashings prostitution
streets removed where once the flinty boots
of workers sparked raw dawn from well-worn cobbles
football fields where Papes and Prods refurbish
the mindless slights of long-abandoned wars . . .

The man at the back of the hall paused to refill his question.

fine buildings have been saved and old slums cleared
we've a ring road the P.S. 'Waverley' the Burrell
the SNO the Citizens Scottish Opera
the countryside around us still unspoiled
most people never see a fight or a drunkard
reeling Fridays off from the calendar
of his memory they're ordinary folk
as decent as they come don't you agree?

Of course, I said: *I agree with every word.*
In fact, I couldn't have put it better myself.

But . . .

II   YOUNG HOMO SAPIENS

Mummy, it says on television that they shoot
animals—sheep and monkeys—through the head
to see what happens when they're not quite dead.
  Please, can you tell me why?

Darling, that isn't just the way to put
it. These dumb creatures feel no pain,
and show what happens to the human brain
  so that brave men won't die.

But mummy, teacher says the dumb brute
is part of God's creation, and that we
must never practise on it cruelty.
  Did teacher tell a lie?

Of course not. Sometimes nations in dispute
can't settle their affairs, so have to kill
each other with the newest guns until
　　the bad are made comply.

But mummy . . . That's enough. Go and compute
the problem on your Spectrum, and then tell
me whatever future it can spell
　　that doesn't scarify.

III   THOUGHT FOR THE DAY

Five hundred helpless foetuses a day,
the woman said in her religious talk—
not soul stuff, but 'The Value of Human Life'—
sucked out of careless womb to surgeon's tray.

What an absurdity when each same day
in jungles, ruined cities, ambushes,
dressed up to kill, men sally out of thought
to murder from, they hope, protective distance!

The world's too full already. There's no room
for the unwanted. Praying doesn't pay:
and, don't forget, the young must have their fling,
believing that The Bomb's their destiny.

Some foetuses, she said, *are heard to cry*
before the silencing incinerator
puts paid to the mistakes they realised
but couldn't understand . . .

Switch the thing off!
What right have they to air such sloppy rubbish?
Has she forgotten all of us must die?
Abortion's just the basic throw-away
of our disposable society.

IV   LONDON CORNER FILLER

Walking, my collar cuffed, down Piccadilly
I look upon a petrified bronze filly,
a naked hairless man astride a horse
gazing at snow, a Force Nine gale, or worse;
and wonder what the other glancers think
of this cold masterpiece by Dame E. Frink.

V   LOST CAUSE

Scotland, the speaker roared, *is a lost cause*
Having allowed my indignation pause
to gather breath, *he's right of course*, I thought.
But so is everything won, sold or bought;
all systems, dogmas, leaky human laws
that can't make music linger past it's close;
protract the flesh's climax; stoke desire
from cooling to affection; hold a pose
that isn't breathing motion; douse the fire
that cringes scent and colour off the rose.

In from some edgeless cold a wind blows.

VI   AUNTIE'S VIEW

I'm fond of Nature programmes, Auntie said—
herds of beasts running the scented air;
fins rippling the balance of hung water;
creatures crawling up their vertical grip;
translucent dazzle probing the sea's bed;
claws scuttling through scratchy clouds of sand.

It's good to get such insight into Nature;
but don't you think it's really rather a bother,
when not being chased or grazing on suspicion,
they're either copulating or eating each other?

VII   A NON-ODE FOR ST ANDREW'S NIGHT

What does tomorrow mean? I asked Sauchiehall Street
one twenty-ninth of November, the microphone
in my hand a smoking gun that shot for answers.
A female giggle, loosely held together,
fluttered free on the wings of vacancy.
It's the night we danced strathspeys and reels in Persia,
though I'm damned if I ever understood quite why,
a commanding voice bluffed through a feathery trail
of conscious English laughter. A sideways queer
veered past: *The night you Scotsmen fling your kilts*
about, and some of us wonder what's underneath.

It's five years to the day since I lost my parrot
and three since my husband died, a crinkly lady
circled, winging off on her own asides.
A self-made top-hat eased out of a Rolls
to throw himself headlong against the question:
Git oot o ma wey oar ahll knoack yir bluidy pan in.
Only a teacher, clipped to the limited flight
of a child's imagination, ventured, qualifying
tentativeness with counter-question: *I think it's*
St Andrew's Night, November thirtieth. Isn't it?
Surely nowadays a meaningless date?

Not much of a bag, I thought, unloading the microphone
into my pocket. But saints no longer fly,
heavy with patronage, over the national sky,
the drone of aircraft making it dangerous.
In a country that has long since jettisoned nationhood,
I should have known better than take pot-shots
at myth, after the bird of purpose has flown.

VIII   IN A GLASGOW LOO

Ah hope yuh dinna mind me speaking tae yi,
sur, but ahve seen youse on the telly? Whit dyuh dae
for a livan? Yuv retired? Yuh wrote? A po-it?
Micht ye no jist as weel hae peed inti thuh wund?

A Birthday Card to Norman MacCaig at Seventy-five

Old conjurer who wears no wizard's hat,
with words for fingers, images for wrists
you juggle up the thought of *this* or *that*,
unknot delight from countless hidden twists,
manipulate a metaphysical *me*
and trick alive what's there, if we could see.

For George Bruce's Eightieth Birthday

You took the whipper-edge of the North East wind,
the blue cold of the sea, of fishermen's jerseys,
the God of testamental storms and plenty,
the glitter of granite and of micaed boxes
slivered full on the scaly quay; lorries
flashing the ways of southern consumption,
and passaged then to poetry: departures
forever charting rocky images
illumined by the lighthouse of the mind.

To Norman Nicholson, 1914–87

They niched you as a 'Christian provincial poet'
in *The Times* obituary. By their way of it
setting you in your place; a small-town museum
musty with broken-backed theology
roofed in with soot blown from the Lancashire mills
when black-cloth pencil figures lent them life,
gardening Lakeland wealth for some, for others
scrimping the threadbare suit of loyalty.

In the flat above the shop, where you were born,
housing invention three and seventy years,
how you'd have huskily laughed! Your love for Millom's
once furnace-lit theatrical skies embraced
the marshy coast, where grease-bound wrack, discarded
by man and sea, dries caked, like scattered nests,
when the high tides draw back their months together;

rains that have washed down age from the Cumbrian fells;
Scafell's rocky brow, now and then baring
its fringe of cloud, scornful as mysticism;
and Wordsworth's River Duddon, talking over
appearance with itself; all it could ever say
till you, dear Norman, riffling time's hair,
a seeming prophet with a kindly air,
looked beyond shroudy mists and crumbling bricks,
looked to the rockland's geological stare;
through such particulars made nature fix
its generalities; identify a voice
divesting absence of its final choice.
Putting a question-mark to certainty,
for whom there was no star on the way back,
you opened the wind's glances—God's curtain,
a stage with no one there to take a bow—
yet made of earth and air and sky the vow
of poetry that outlives all personal lack:
thanks be for that, the only why or how;
thanks be for that, poet, forever and now.

Burying a Friend

Death, I have always pushed you to the back
of the mind's queue, believing that the strength
of my concerns would shield me from attack,
what lay between us making such a length
of interests; the instincts of the pack
thickening safety with the human need
to lunge along the scent that lured the track,
whoever faltered in the long stampede.
Now, I've outrun that distance; won the lack
of future possibilities, so pour
over a backward-reaching almanac
with only space for guessing up my score;
the queue so short I doubt I'll even see
you, Death, come closing to unnumber me.

Dona Nobis Pacem

The crematorium chimney thumbs
smudges like clouds; a smoky smear
daubing the vacancies of heaven,
that telephone exchange of prayer,
connecting—where? Beyond Neptune,
blue with its backwards, gassy moon
meandering round the solar edge
from which the guttering stars recede,
leaving their emptied light behind,
a scattering of celestial crumbs?

What out there could possibly heed
the little warmth we briefly wear,
whatever from, however given,
that only answers breathing's need?

Echoes of fervent words we find
rung back, calling our inner ear;
yet even a sound that seems to share
itself brings consolation of a kind.

The Palace of Varieties
Six Songs from an Imaginary Review

I *SECULAR SERMON SONG*

Go down Moses, you scary prophet man;
since beards went out of fashion they're not a source of truth;
your tablets are all broken; it's catch-as-catch-can
in a world that's full of sayers with precious little sooth.

Go down Moses. The rushes whisper spies;
the cloud of God's unknowing protects no promised land
and heaven fires the innocent whom gunmen terrorise
with absolutes that welter, but actions countermand.

Go down Moses. The Sea's no more divide,
and those who think they're chosen simply look absurd;
the air-space over mountain-tops affords no exit ride
now faith's self-martyrdom and multi-colours blur The Word.

According to determinists—and you were one of those—
the conflicts and catastrophes that rake our daily lives
are fixed by the environment and genes we didn't choose;
so, Moses, heads you just can't win and tails you're bound to lose.

But what's it really matter? We've strained past breaking point
the uselessness of pity, so up Jack's ladder pulled.
When lambs make tainted mutton there's nothing to anoint;
the genie's out the bottle and can't be overruled.

II POP SONG

I think my body hates me, a multi-millionaire
whose money doesn't buy the how to make things less unfair.
At twenty-one I've made the grade, yet run beyond the post
of where I thought was winning, yet feels as if it's lost.
I thrive on raw sensation, and strive to be its edge;
the higher up the mountain, the narrower the ledge
to rest your laurels on, look back and wonder who comes next,
with every challenge clobbered and all the fixers fixed.
My hour has gone, as pop stars go, but climbing all the way
from kitchened slum to glitzyland, I won't resign my day.
For still the youngters chart me; with sensualising hips
I slaver at the microphone from gashed-with-crimson lips.
I've powdered my complexion till the skin absorbs no more;
I look half like a circus clown and half a windowed whore.
My lyric lisp suggestiveness through noise of every kind
that leans against a whisper and isn't high on mind.
I've homes in thirteen countries, yet in whichever one
I lodge, I'm served with loneliness when all the shouting's done
and teenager hysterics are wrapped in pimply beds
to dream of being safely made suburban newly weds.
I've hooked myself on fashionable drugs, and paid the price—
a reputation punctured by featured media vice—
I've had sex in every continent of Venus; multi-angled
in positional varieties where I've been nearly strangled
till sight and smell of naked flesh congeals exhausted dust
with nothing in its taste or touch to move me love or trust.
Surely my body hates me, with nothing left to try
but hype it past the limits of what it's like to die?

III HOODLUM'S HUM

I don't want to light a flame in your heart,
baby, I want to set the world on fire;
through terror cause Establishments abort;
melt supermarkets; gut the cackling spire
of town hall and cathedral, till they snort
confusion as the fearful sparks fly higher:
  old ways make laws to halt the new;
  bullets proclaim what's overdue.

The hour has struck for those who, masked like me,
are saviours of the world and meet the bill
with slit-eyed murder; force The People free,
since blood's the sacrificial thing to spill,
especially from those who won't agree;
however bluffed the call, I shoot to kill.
  But while we wait for Kingdom Come,
  disposable baby, serve me dumb.

IV SCOTTISH NATIONAL SONG

Land of our birth we pledge to thee, I remember singing
as a small boy in the school's assembly hall,
our love and toil in the years to be; the bright words ringing
up images of knight-errantry, ideal over all.
Half-a-century on, I know that such a concept
hasn't cash value, can't rate stocks and shares,
any more than eternal love's irredeemable vows are kept
beyond the quarrel flung down a tenement stairs.

Instead, we've toiled to sell our land to the highest bidder,
packaging *Scotland the Brave* for marauding money men;
of self-sufficiency determined to rid her
for a generationful of dollars or yen.
At last, *Will Ye No Come Back Again?*, has got its answer;
there's nobody waiting now to be summoned by yells
from foreign football fields, or the songs of the kilted romancer—
only an aimless wind blows through abandoned shells.

V PROVERBIAL SONG

Somebody dropped a stitch-in-time
and ripped the other running nine;
the stone that stayed to gather moss
found itself insulating loss;
the many-a-slip twixt cup-and-lip
uncounted chicks that seemed a snip;
the true words spoken oft in jest
turned every worst a loser's best;
the bird-in-hand squeezed up a push
and joined the others in the bush;
pride failed to go before its fall,
he who laughed last laughed not at all
and every pickle near the knuckle
unmade some canny Scotsman's puckle;
chipping the old block lost its knack.

Pull up the ladder, all-right Jack,
for what's it matter in the end
when life's one long make-do-and-mend?

VI A SONG TO MYSELF

It's Cabaret Time, shouts the compère, blond and poncey
as the band blares out a fanfare, phoney as flat champagne;
and a bevy of girls, half naked and over sonsie,
in case you misheard, shriek: *It's Cabaret Time* again.

Time to give over sonnets in regular measure;
Time to forget you're no longer righter than rain;
Time to remember the wings of the dove of pleasure
that fluttered your heart and flattered your ageing pen.

Laugh at the best, and the rest, of what floats before you;
drama giocosa, the *comédie humaine*;
though its errors and terrors distress you, they never bore you;
you may wince at the chorus as long as you laugh at the pain.

Lehar's Vienna

They dance the years in evening dress or furs;
money is not a problem; protocol
demands a stud whose blood's as rich as hers,
the heart that dares presume a lover's role
swirled through a three-four slow melodic rinse
till lo! poor Mr Wrong's a rightful prince.

What would they do if they should twirl beyond
the footlight's reach? Go nakedly to bed
where, long before a top-lit morning dawned,
he'd pleasure off the family maidenhead?
Then swelling pregnancy and parturition,
the fruiting that is beauty's full condition?

Oh no! They're not like us, illusion's creatures
whose dreamy turnings time has left unstilled,
anticipation eagering their faces
though guns and tanks go breeding, Jews get killed;
trapped by the bars that only keep you humming,
they cast no shadow and hold no becoming.

Requiem for a Sexual Athlete

He was married ten times, losing six wives by divorce and three by death. Obituary on a
film composer, *The Times*, 18.4.87.

She sits herself down opposite you on a train;
you notice the flashed curves of her crossed legs
calyxing shadowed promise under the skirt.
Thinking *millions of others are better* begs
the question you hear your body's lust blurt
to a mind that answers hopefully: *God! Not again.*

She leans to ease her jacket off, the thrust
of her breasts so deep the finial nipples show,
her narrow waist bent steep on the bough of her hips.
Rapping your fingering eyes, she adjusts her *no-
go* look; but, curiously, she flips
round the magazine edge of an agony aunty's decent trust.

Though ceaselessly the life force churns and burns,
and it's words and woods away since Adam seeded Eve,
or Tarzans plucked fresh Janes from passing trees,
for you, with a hungry animal ego hard to please
and a carefully tailored heart pinned to your sleeve,
it's the taming of flesh on which the challenge turns.

As each new she peels off her shyness, sighs
submission to your body's hard impress,
the facelessness of sex lies stretched beneath
you: comforting breasts; encircling legs; a sheath
to drain your own inadequacies; less
and less the singular one you schemed to hypnotise.

Orchestrator of larger-than-life emotion;
the focuser of cinema dark where feeling's believing;
where heroines play forever hard to get,
and heroes, over-accustomed to handsomeness, never set
down macho; even when the audience is leaving,
braced for the touch of night's abrasive lotion

that cleanses off an evening out's illusion;
heading for home's acceptable conventions—
cross children, dirty dishes, the scurry of bills—
a vacuumed expectation that dailyness fills
with stronger bonds than the tuneless sexual tensions
snapping your screwed-up strings, *da-capo*-ing confusion.

Variations and Fugue on a Christmas Tune

1

Stille nacht, heilige nacht . . . the strain
of the old Austrian carol bumbles out
from a brass band; a colding month's refrain
as soldiers of the Sally Army tout
for charity among the well-heeled crowd
hurrying gift-wrapped parcels homewards, bright
with Christmas feelings raucously aroused
as TV shepherds flock their sales by night.

Struggling for Christ beneath a Bible sun,
from murdered innocence a soldier darts
through cornered ruins guarded by a gun
to snipe at hatred in opposing hearts,
or stop a bullet marked with Allah's name—

What fictive star would stop for us again?

2

Stille nacht, heilige nacht . . . the canned sound
seeps through the jostling store. One of the crowd
senses it vaguely; like the frosty ground
outside, or the swaddled manger tinselling the shroud
beside an empty tomb. Words, like bricks
from the toy counter, easily structure a faith
each con-man dogmas out with his own tricks
of the true believer's stock-in-trade. Thus saith . . .
Well, who? God, Allah, Buddha? Each one picks
according to his fantasy or fear.
The only gifts we get are birth and death.

Why shape miracles out of a myth's ear?

3

Stille nacht, heilige nacht, a music-box trickles
through the steamed window-heat of celebration.

The moon cuts silhouettes from daylight's patterns;
creatures breathe out cartoons of speech that don't get filled;
fields of frost are ground keen to the edge for sowing.

Fragments of shattered firmaments
signal to earth's stability.

Sssh . . . till . . . eh . . . the clockwork gasps
against another year's unwinding.

Supposing the balance slipped,
this honing cold cut more than scraped for growing,
grazed the skin of the atmosphere, thinning
Shakespeare, Mozart, the warmth of loving,
the flesh and thresh of sex, our rationales
of hatred, slackening speculations, prices,
and politicians' promises . . . promises . . .

What price a legendary manger then?

4

First voice:
We've come a long say from the way it was
beneath the tumbled jostle of history
that can't add credit to an improbable cause,
or lend us means to measure a mystery.

Second voice:
So much confusion, such brittle men of the hour;
a Church that buttressed the wealthy and the State
with pomp and circumstance of temporal power;
a far cry for the beggar at the gate.

Third voice:
Licentious Romans marshalling tribal Jews
gave place to monks and myths in the Dark Ages;
then primavera sunshine rose to suffuse
a golden world whose bright enamelled pages
torturing bigots tore apart, misused
for lighting fires to warm sectarian rages.

Fourth voice:
Inquisition crept in like a thief
to steal the tortured conscience of belief.

First voice:
All that was long ago. A little nearer,
though smalling now, those sentimental sages,
Victorian prophets, preaching that none were ever clearer
how orders should be fixed, which deaths were sin's wages.

Second voice:
Two wars shattered more than complacent trust.
Who can keep faith with pointless millions dead,
forget the Holocaust and re-adjust
the price of the wine of blood and the flesh of bread?

Third voice:
So here we are, near the twentieth century's end;
the cut-price century that invented annihilation;
did what the other animals only pretend,
unstoppering a brand new plague in celebration.

Fourth voice:

The star we followed hovers us over Aids,
and the wise men bring, not gifts, but anxious chatter
on how to defeat the latest in human dreads
while the less than wise pretend that it doesn't matter.

First voice:
Words, words; from politician and priest,
rearranging impossibilities;
no longer the first shall be last, but the last shall be least;
to each, according to his credit facilities.

Second voice:
Like it or not, now is the time for greetings;
for rhyming robins on hollied sledges dropping
through letterboxes; office parties; reunion meetings;
the time for spending on lending, for Christmas shopping.

Third voice:
For the chaste and the unchased huntresses of counters,
breasting through seas of satisfaction where bargains lie;
housewives, fiancées, mothers; the great surmounters
always knowing for whom and what to buy.

Fourth voice:
Brimmings of warmth in the heart and anxious skimmings
of past years' lists and parcel wrapping out of the way,
it's time to think of the turkey and the trimmings;
the tiffs of relations, the touchiness of friends;
those for whom peace on earth, it seems, never quite
descends;
who's fallen out with whom; who's coming on the day.

Fourth voice:
It's important we don't sit thirteen round the table,
or so my great, great grandmother used to say.

First voice:
But we're not superstitious . . .

Second voice:
                    . . . we're never able
to think our number's unluckier than another's.

Third voice:
At least we try to make sure that we haven't lost
the Christmas spirit commercialisation smothers.

Fourth voice:
Giving, receiving gifts, as if the cost
hadn't been jangled for weeks on the television screen.

First voice:
Surely these actors can't believe what they mean?

Second voice:
Or is it the TV glass that opaques between
false messages that fade with the morning frost?

First and second voices:
We both adore the carols; that Austrian thing
sugar-plum fairies coat on the crib of heaven,
set up in the market place where people bring
the random change that slotted charity's given.

Third and fourth voices:
The sawdust-smelling glare of the circus ring
we treat the family to on Christmas Eves;
then home to the off-to-sleep and the tip-toe Santa thing.

Stretto:
No matter how fundamentally each of us disbelieves
in tales first told to make primitive tribes submit
to a monarch's rule of fear; in a virgin who conceives
so that guilt's ground into sexual love like the grit
of ages; or we, like most, think of the vacancy of hereafter
a self-preserving trick of the prideful mind,
this Winter Solstice is a time for laughter;
for thanking the stars that seem in place, but unwind
backwards through light and distance, leaving us behind
to be kind to ourselves and each other, filled with our human
   cheer
on Christmas night, the first night of the resurrecting year.

Out There

Watching the news on TV smooth the face
of high-jack, air disaster, hundreds dead,
across the floor I sensed a shadow race
to squeeze behind my feet some mortal dread
before the glaring teeth from which it fled.
My curt command cut short the feline chase;
the trembling fur I lifted scarcely bled,
a matted leg the worst that I could trace.

Watching my rabbit freed, through long grass run
back to its menaced freedom, I returned
to how, instead of teeth, the bomb and gun
now lacerate a larger innocence, spurned
by every dogma-eaten fanatic
who thinks cold blood can make a bad cause stick.

Old Boys

How are you keeping? Casually we meet,
childhood familiars in an ageing street.
As fit's to be expected, he replies.
With bland uncaring, each of us then vies
self-thankfulness; for nothing so annoys
a chap as when some fellow over-spills
his littleness of long-imagined ills.
You're looking healthy too, politeness claims,
recalling those afflicted; some, dead names.
We separate our ways. I laugh like hell,
two ancient boys, so singularly well!

Overseas Departure Lounge

Leaving behind the levitating years
of staying at the top—the push, like battle,
that forced his sales advance; thrombotic fears
take-over rumours threatened; the low rattle
of board-room knives on busy luncheon plates
(which blandly munching face the dangerous one?),
sleek secretaries flexing endless dates—
he sold his shares and settled for the sun.

Casting the neat ambitions that had numbed
him, basked in shorts and browner than the sand,
the only driving force he still succumbed
to, daily golf with one of the band;
then toddling to the British Club for drinks,
to hear once more what everybody thinks.

Framed

Glancing out from the window of a train
I saw a scarecrow lying on its back,
denting the ripened waviness of grain
it stood to guard before the wind's attack;
the body, propped on pole-arms, seemed to bloat:
two crows sat pecking at its turnip cheeks,
while others ripped its Charlie Chaplin coat
of stuffing, clacking bright triumphant beaks.
A nightmare's ballad-image, I'd suppose;
except that scarecrow soldiers, stiff with fear,
nightly go stalking causes others chose,
enfoliaged in the latest killing gear,
between the TV feature and football,
stumbling to where they too are carrion sprawl.

The Non-Achiever

What do you mean to do with your life?, the headmaster asked;
the mumbled answer didn't really know;
except, he wanted to be one of those who basked,
like firthing sharks, in success's easy flow.
Somewhere along the road, he took a wrong turning,
no certain signpost looming up to show
him which way wishes went, or where lay warning
            an old man's age ago.

He did his best to defy the rod tradition
that reared him never to except too much;
to regard the naked senses with suspicion;
or, better still, to look but not to touch.
An elder of the Kirk, the president of societies,
he smiled on those whose weakness made him rich;
the mistresses he stripped avoided notorieties;
ambiguously master of dubieties,
            he'd jump the broadest ditch.

Then, on the other side, feel somehow foxed,
what he'd pursued bolt-holing from a mind
that never feared the coursing, nor got boxed
in by old difficulties, nor led from behind.
Yet tails or heads, with women as with horses, action
for its own make-or-break, the profitably lined
take-over balance, proved alike distraction:
at the forbidden core of each bared satisfaction
there was simply nothing to find.

Ports of Call

I JANUARY: VISITING EXMOOR

We stood, the group of us, conservationists
out to preserve unspoiled the little we can
of wilderness places. Above us, Exmoor mists
unspun their thinness. Suddenly, sunlight ran
through the Doone Gate. My literary mind
focused on fictional passions long ago;
a girl who was never one of her family's kind;
a man for whom love would only have her so.
This peat is smooth as butter, the expert said;
taste it. As I spat out the simile, my far
binoculars ranged on an upturned sheep, its head
sightless though moving a little, a red scar
trickling its milky udders beneath the squat
of a raven. Disgust and a strange fear
shuddered me, till the others' friendly looks
returned me the familiar now and here
that reason shapes, and thought defines in books.

The moorland stretched its distance; silent, clear . . .

Three training fighters screamed across a bluff,
trailing their scorch of menace like a scuff.

II FEBRUARY: THE VIETNAM MEMORIAL, WASHINGTON DC

Marshalled platoons of tourists troop to see
this gestured ceremonial public loss:
while peasants learn to live with what they must,
here, downed as if by flak, a grounded V
lies sunk in its uncastellated fosse,
staring its lists of bleak dismembered trust.

When menace leans beyond its emphasis
and leaders borrow lives to flesh their need
upholding the abstraction of a cause,
one side or the other comes to this.
The future cocks an ear that both must heed
if they would win posterity's applause,

claim cynics. But we know, less well-deceived,
the just can't always mollify their aims.
So the stone mourns the father, husband, son
in gleaming mindless glory, state-conceived,
while we mourn corporate numbers, not the names,
where some stand numbly, eyes only for one.

III MARCH: MOCKING BIRD, HOUSTON, TEXAS

Branching the earthy lightness of his claws
upon a TV aerial, he unfolds
his borrowed repertoire, without applause
or varying the fragile clutch he holds
on multi-channelled masquerading choice;
he doesn't try to sell you fashioned things,
but runs his mocking through, voice after voice,
till, coming on his own again, unclings,
having fulfilled the present of his cause,
and crumples silence underneath his wings.

IV APRIL: THE UNITED NATIONS BUILDING, NEW YORK

1

Inside the United Nations building
we're shown the empty-circled luxury
where the ambassadors of nations meet,
deliberate on how to make self-interest
appear disinterested, and clap a veto
on any awkward-running consequence:
but where, 'jaw-jaw' being better than 'war-war',
they vote and then agree to disagree.

2

A piece of moon set in a magnified
glass prism—brownish granite flecked with white—
that multi-racial tourists, who, by night
looked up and listened as their language lied—
green cheese; Diana, huntress chaste and fair;
silvering terrors from its darker side;
the tensions that resolve a woman's tide;
the magnet of the slavering madman's stare—
now marvel that a weightless astronaut
should chip myth to a pocketful of rock;
tossed lava, cooled within the spatial lock
that holds our crumb of earth, and all we've got;
then shuffle off on feet a trifle sore
to seek a pee or find the exit door.

3

Outside, in a plot of dusty bushes,
five sparrows circle, settle for a spar,
raising their squeaky voices, clacking beaks;
something to do with territoriality
or tribal rites. The argument succeeds,
and each returns its separate direction,
miniaturising moments out of weeks.

V MAY: VIENNA

A fat tenor sobbing monocled dreams
to uncomprehending childhood; my father's
Sunday gramophone lilting *Lilac Time*,
a sweetened Spring proclaiming heliotrope;
earth raining vain anonymity
on Mozart's coffin, dumped in a pauper's grave;
the astonished look torn from the shot face
of a Pocket Chancellor anschlussed with death;
an exaggerated peak cap and moustache
gliding through hands that shaped bread, made love,
yet stretch up for a Jew-hate benediction.

Fifty years on, I step from a sleeping-car,
glints of Rhine and Danube edging the drawn
blinds of the night I've left as far behind as the Channel,
anticipation, fresh as the new morning.

What did I expect? What do I find?

Tourists clopping open fiacres,
cabbies pointing up the neo-Baroque
Franz Joseph's fading pictures celebrate;
shops that afford an easy affluence;
coffee and Mozart-kügeln; the worn strains
of a Danube long since rinsed of its waltzing blue.

Some are still Nazis under the skin, they say;
beneath slapped leder-hosen, dirndled charm,
and music leafing memory everywhere.

Sipping my streetwise leisure in a cafe,
I watch the weathered smiles, the handsome bronze
Grüss Gotts, the lively beer, the relaxed air . . .

Which of us knows what history can't disarm?

VI *JUNE: THE BEACH AT ARROMANCHES, NORMANDY*

Difficult now to imagine the wading men
burdened with fear and weapons as a hail
of gunfire spurted the still-defended span
of the bomb-lit, softened beachhead; shell upon shell
crumping the ruins of this seaside town;
the enemy line stretched to its bursting zenith;
the arrowing invasion thrusting on,
its crumpled corpses left, at one with death.
A fortieth summer shines; the same sea glints
with bathers' shouts and bouncing coloured boats;
the waves the swimmers breast give little dunts
against the crusted pontoons no tide lifts.
But fields of crosses, the crop of liberty,
stand harvestless beneath the rescued sky.

VII *JULY: CASABLANCA*

In the train from Marakesch to Casablanca,
first class, uneasily through twenty centuries
I look out on half desert; shifted contours
of dusty sand loose-folded by the wind
for ease of picking up in lazy rises.

Men, dumped in loosely-hanging loneliness,
from *there* to *there* jog little donkeys; patient
with burdened promise, robed in bible myth,
past buildings crouched in straggled squats of palm-trees
where bright-robed bosses banter solicitudes.

I look out on a fragment, isolated
as a painting or a previous century's poem,
a story heard and tabletted in heaven
where poverty's the only tokened grace
with which the barely-living buy off death.

An arab waiter's spicy buns and coffee
serve to remind me I, at least, am travelling
nearer to filmed-up sleazy Casablanca;
back to my total absence of belief.

The engine, shuffling faster, hoots relief.

VIII   AUGUST: DUBROVNIK

In Dubrovnik, an old man said to me:
here, we have learned not to be bound
by things which there is a need to define.
Under Capitalism, man exploits man;
the same thing happens under Socialism,
only the other way round. So, you see,
I am simply a seller of wine.

IX   SEPTEMBER: ST TROPEZ

A Van Gogh sun itches across the skies,
reddening stretched-out strips of nakedness;
juicing the downy grapes in green-hung fields
behind the port where money-makers' cruisers
drowsily nod, white sterns bobbing the quayside
ready to slip to sea should millions beckon.

Bottles and glasses glint a cooler welcome
from under street-side café awnings. Ageing
painterly men daub turpsy images,
mixing abandoned styles with poster fancies,
memorials to fade on foreign walls.

Pleasures beguile. A fully opened light
lets sea and shore and verdant hills relax
within its azure gap. Across the gulf,
the Mistral breathes a warning, summer's harm.

Only the swallows flirt with vague alarm.

X   OCTOBER: A CHURCH IN FRANCE

A fine exterior, the guidebook said;
and so it was, the soft Romanesque curls
still clutching life, though features that once pled
for urgency had whitened into whorls
powdered with time. Small groups of tourists strolled
vaguely in admiration; others, less
concerned than with the noise the traffic hauled
through briefly intermingled purposes.

A thickened peasant woman, widow-laired,
creaked the door open. Sheltered darkness smelt
of mustiness. A gantried corner flared
its guttering candles. There, the woman knelt
with others fixed in ritualistic pose.

But as I watched, their faces seemed to run
to vacant anonymity, as those
on the stone arch long since had done,
past which the squaling drone of traffic rolled
as, fretting in its tower, a lone bell tolled.

XI   NOVEMBER: AT DELPHI

I quaffed a sook o thon Castallian spring
on Mount Parnassus. It cam gushan oot
freely frae some un-Apollonian thing,
a wabbit-luikan dug-like metal spoot.
For lang eneuch I hesitatit, foot
upon the haly hill sacred tae verse;
But ilka time I stoopt, a bus wuld toot
and gar me strauchtan my poetic erse.
At last I thocht: *I wullna gie a hoot*,
and bendan doun my heid, gulpit a scoosh.
Ae minute later I'd a soakan suit,
shoved intil't by anither bus's whoosh.
It seems in these days aince respecktit Goades
are nae sae weil-regairdit as fast roads.

XII   DUDDINGSTON LOCH, NOW AND THEN

Mufflered figures lean on their gravity
through curves that trace on ice a kind of speech
spelling out crunch, yet uttered with a suavity
that dry-land keeps stonily out of reach.

Photographs in an album, frozen pages
of wintered waters, once a memo pad
scribbled with cold forgotten messages
from skaters in now-lost conventions clad.

To-day repeats those hieroglyphics, freed
of period, meaning, measure or command;
as if some god of skaters had agreed
to sign such pleasure with a hasty hand
before the gathered brows of clouds could mass
to wipe its brittle clamour clear as glass.

Late Spring

Daffodils raise trumpets, as to order; purse lips
and, braced against the veers of April, blow
the hope renewal brings. Buds that were sticky tips
swelling their wintered boughs—which, lately, snow
picked out in thickened whiteness—suddenly let go,
scattering husks to loosen the felicity
that greens them to a bosomed overflow
of blossom; as a lover gently slips
into delight and sweet lubricity.

For me, Spring's now a kind of raree-show
exciting backward marvel. Thorned with age's treason,
I'm not involved in nature's sexual complicity
of opulence to breast time into season.

Regret's the last dry flourish to outgrow.

An Elegy for Leon, The Brindled Bouvier
(age 3½, dead of a heart attack)

Man is the dog's god
                Burns

Last thing at night I opened the front door;
dazily from his human fireside doze
my dog leapt out and rushed off to explore
the ancient world he brushed with his black nose;

a map of sniffs and scents beneath the ground—
signals, faint shuffles that I couldn't hear—
while I, supposedly the more profound,
gazed upwards at a sky filled far and near

with burnt-out proclamations of infinity.
Doubting his local darkness, green eyes stared
for reassurance, while this dog's divinity
pondered the *why* of breath we briefly shared.

The Groves of Academe

At school, he was known as 'the great beast of swot',
never quite clear of a dose of dust-in-the-head,
or that it was only itself the past taught,
saying it over again when nothing more's to be said.

At university, he followed the rules
laid down by the professors of perdition,
his mind, a tape-machine recording spools
of images in umpteenth-hand condition,

but correct in every dotted *i*, stroked *t*.
With a first in English, the question then arose,
so stuffed with knowledge, what would he like to be?
Nothing, he reckoned, that could possibly expose

him to the contagious dailyness of living.
With everything recorded, the tape wound back,
to future generations he'd go on giving
immaculate accounts of his own lack.

A sound man in his subject, the obiturist said,
if a trifle unoriginal. I stared at the sight
of the worn features I'd thought of as years-ago dead,
reflecting, how wrong was *The Times*, and I, how right.

A Wedding

I THE CROWD BEFORE

Anything makes a passing crowd gawp;
a dog run over by a bus, a fight
between two drunks. People will simply stop
if you look up at some imagined flight
and gaze along with you, hoping some sop
to dailyness has swum into your sight.
Nothing so makes a busy woman drop
her purpose, as a bride, arrived in white.
My, she's luvely, a leather-skinned old dear
proclaims. Another sighs: *She disnae ken
that things'll no turn oot as they appear.
A wumman cannae pit her trust in men.*
Most hoped that for this union just begun,
love would do more than it for them had done.

II THE MOTHER

It's all been worth it. How radiantly sweet
she looks there, leaning on her father's arm!
The Wedding March half-turns her glance to greet
her chosen. Oh the indescribable charm
of youth, believing it can last the heat
of the day, with no presentiment of harm,
as on it goes to find its own defeat;
experience; the middle years' alarm!
She'll be all right till the children are growing up
and he starts undressing dollies on the side;
whatever you try, however hard you hope,
you're parted; an invisible divide
leaves neither of you with that much to say;
and you know that life has somehow lost your way.

III   THE FATHER

Fixed in his plumping morning suit, and proud
to have two thousand friends—well, guests—in the kirk
the silvered hymn-sheets filling it with the loud
praise that sustained him—just another perk
success brought with it—gratefully, he bowed
before the altar; he, the one-time clerk
whose dullard school-days muddied through a cloud,
whose chauffeur smirked beside a smiling Merc.
What if the guy she'd chosen was a jerk?
Surely at least he had sufficient guile
to make himself essential at his work
for long enough to let him heap his pile?
Meanwhile, a wilful daughter, safely wed,
would tame to domesticity in bed.

IV   THE BRIDE

Beneath her blouse the cup of his hand on her breast,
or tensing where the touch of pleasure is—
till they were married, she'd withheld the rest,
however much he huffed or took it amiss;
a man should marry a virgin, her mother impressed
upon her, though all she wanted was to be his,
reason and fear and bashfulness undressed
to take him into her submissiveness.
So, at the altar, formalised and cool,
she swore to love him, honour and obey,
accepting the Middle Class's social rule
she'd doubts about: it seemed the simplest way
to reach their fleshs' two-in-one release,
transforming baulked desire to lovers' peace.

V   THE BRIDEGROOM

Well, yes, he'd loved her; wanted her for keeps;
not one of the ready girls he'd laid in town
for the price of drinks and a dinner, but who sleeps
with a profession. One to be his own
he'd come to fathom to the ultimate deeps
of what there was to know, and not be blown
off course by argument or womanly weeps.
He'd find time, too, for kids, however pressing
the bosses turned their tightening business screw;
and sex always to hand would be a blessing,
without the time-consuming need to woo;
yet if things went awry . . . well wasn't it true,
easily off with the old and on with the new?

VI   THE MINISTER

His cassock, like his platitudes, shabbily smooth
since reasoned age had forced on him a weaning
from dogma's milk that nobody could prove
sustained the truth which kept the faithful preening
themselves, and made proverbial mountains move;
though still he shuttled words from which his gleaning
had long receded—a clickity-clacking groove
that wove a shapeless fabric of unmeaning—
what did it matter? Innocents were born,
and needed names to mark their earthly span,
or marry. If no everlasting morn
awoke them out of death, why, not a man
returned to say the whole thing was a fraud.
He blessed this couple in the name of God.

VII   THE BEST MAN

Feeling the ring in his pocket, the draft of his speech,
and awkward, hired to a suit that didn't quite fit,
sideways he glanced at the bridesmaid: rather a peach,
depending on whether you were a leg or a tit
man; in due course, he hoped to be able to reach
his own conclusions, when the Reception lit
up later. But here was the Minister starting to preach!
(He blushed that his sexy thoughts made him feel such a git!)
After the frozen photographs by the door
of the church, the telegrams' risqué jokes,
and some desultory shuffling round a floor
the size of a rug with their vaguely related folks,
he held his partner's bodice, but not her mind,
for they were simply two of a different kind.

VIII   THE BRIDESMAID

Would it be her turn next? Or was she too choosy?
So many men were only after the thing
all women possessed, the duchess and the floosy.
Those that she'd thought had qualities to bring
to a life together, turned out to be boozy
and unreliable. You could have your fling
with another girl, of course; or marry a snoozy
older man, if security needed a ring.
She wanted a chap with something fresh to say;
who'd read a bit; been around, and listened and seen
what mattered; so that, come the close of the day,
she wouldn't be bored. How had the Best Man been?
One who talked of himself, like ephemeral pop:
the kind of fellow who didn't know where to stop.

IX   THE GRANDPARENTS

For better or for worse brightly they vow,
thrilled with the promises of young desire.
Forever's not like honey-tasting now;
yet we dare hope that when their bodies tire,
and age rules worry on the other's brow,
they'll hold together through the thickening mire
of middle life and find that when they row,
the strongest forging's from the hottest fire.
Experience grows closer with the wearing;
so long as separate faults are left ignored,
two minds grow linked in telepathic sharing
a sympathy through love that's well explored;
accepting the returns of give and take,
you get the kind of happiness you make.

X   THE CROWD AFTER

My, she's a picture, the crowd says in *oo*'s,
as, arm-in-arm, the newly-weds appear;
their happiness, the stuff of youth to use
for pleasuring each other in a here-
and-now that passion will suffuse
with wonder as they each-to-each cohere,
their daily world, a little thing to lose
since love like theirs could not be priced too dear.
The crowd, aware that love's a pretty ruse
to people nature, loosens up a cheer.
They'd do it all again, if they could choose
to run another round, renew their year
like Christmas; the illusion of beginning,
with odds, however long, on this time winning.

Animal Rights Man Eating Out

This table suit you, sir? the waiter, bored,
welcomed the man in dim cathedral gloom.
The menu's bad-French litany explored,
the diner glanced across the crowded room,

a daylight tank, its opalescent glare
rilling its bubbled water where, claws bound,
blue flecked with white and bead-eyed vacant stare,
a clutch of lobsters scrabbled glassy ground,

or lay half-sleeping, waving antennae
not fashioned to encounter slides like this
where starers peer and then identify
one chosen for the boiling water's hiss.

Watching a lobster-chooser dithering—
'we have to eat: the good Lord made it so'—
he fancied that he saw him slithering,
plucked from the pile when his turn came to go

and, fully clothed, be plunged in bibled flames
well-cooked to conscience red, the full amount.
But no! He's back to prattling business aims
since culinary killing 'doesn't count.'

Seeing's Believing?

Catarrh that muffled in from the Atlantic
muggered the hills and sagged the central plain,
weather-forecasted, the prevailing antic
to-morrow, cloudy again with occasional rain.

It's clogged my ears and given me Berkeley's Balance—
nothing is there but what you happen to see—
the world's hung out, a dazzling ziggered valance,
colours that run where the edges ought to be.

Reading between the lines, a sideways V
opens its jaws to snap up common sense,
while hostile furniture prances, cap-a-pie
and *here*, so far as I'm concerned, has become *hence*.

It's like being forced to live out carnival, where
spatial relationships break the dividing fence;
the ride whirls on till its nothing everywhere,
the inverse of a carnival's controlled pretence.

My doctor slows down the roller-coaster sway
with pills and rest and drops to sniff up the nose;
but how in the world, on an ordinary day,
can we know what's there, or what other eyes compose?

As If It Mattered

He's a forties poet, the eighties critic said.
Perhaps I am. What difference does it make?
Decades divide the living, not the dead;
and poetry's an urging youth can't slake.

Eventually, the hounds of period-savour,
sniffing their way through thickets of neglect,
yelp with discovery, bear you back to favour,
a contentious bone of academic respect;

a peg in the grudging cloakroom of Scottish fame;
PhD subject someone blithely elects
to shape into a handle for his name;
or punctuation a textual scholar dissects.

For a time your reputation loses face,
but the poetry remains to testify—
the resurrection Spring puts back in place;
young love's first fingers on a startled thigh;
a cut of swallows mesmerising sky;
the changelessness that history doesn't trace—
when fashion's frumped and can't keep up the pace.

Living By Water

What makes us want to live beside water,
the looking-glass of space, the vacant eye
that stares the sun back at its own blind game?
Fretted, we say it scuds or suds with laughter,
but, raging in destruction, wonder why
the difference of touching wears no name.

So we make friends with it on our own terms,
searching dry land for the world's regard—
the which, if we can find it, proves to be
a temporary bind against the harms
that eat away the fabric of reward,
like termites, or the washing of the sea.

Salty or fresh, blocked ice, revolving rain,
water retains its own identity,
mimicking moods and seasons by the way,
as thought dissolves into itself again
and we stay land-locked in sufficiency
till death froths off the surface of our day.

What's Yours?

Abstracts and absolutes; the great and good
vacuities before which vanities kneel,
cushioning fancy in an attitude
that makes us sure we're greater than we feel;
contentious superstition that proclaims
a single truth and gluts upon the greed
of certainty (the abstract no word shames,
the measureless sad strain of human need).

Abstracts and absolutes; protected, shown
illusory on television screens;
accorded dignities their deeds disdain,
their ceremonies, ends without the means,
sinking horizons deep in sightless death;
their promises, an endless whiff of bliss
that you can only pay for with your breath;
hereafter's world made out of dreams from this.

The gods are dead! one self-made leader cries
equality's the substance of the State;
statistics, numbers, not old feudal lies;
it's corporate effort that you must equate
with bourgeois longings, personal desires
and spiritual bunkum, History's passed
you by; consign it to the cleansing fires;
cure the romantic agony at last.

Alive on time, like any well-run show,
a white-winged surplice flutters humbleness
as he, on earth God's first man in the know,
kisses the ground, crosses the air to bless
arenas banked with cheers, then touches heads
with benediction charged to countermand
the ruin of the world that living spreads,
the symbol of belief, his mortal hand.

Across the vultured frontier, turbaned age,
the bones of barbarism picked for text,
thunders severer prophecies; a rage
of vengeance downed on those whose thoughts have vexed
Mohammed, voicing God's recorded word,
a tape the endless sun loops daily through.

Abstracts and absolutes, alike absurd,
your time's gone past; we should have done with you,
dogmas brawling the streets of the mind like strumpets . . .

Ha, ha, the horse still saith among the trumpets.

Flight 143, New Orleans to Houston

You see them fields of stone-like boxes, the man said
as he drove me to the airport, *side by side?*
That's the Nu Orluns way we bury our dead.
After a year, we can open them up and slide

another body in. The heat of the sun's so great,
there's nuthun left but dust. I paid my fare,
checked in my flight, and settled down to wait—
what a mix of vanished skills the dust must share!

Marshalled, I'm roared away on the jet's protrusive thrust;
smalling beneath, the bayou's lead-eyed swamps,
the balconied French Quarter's delicate crust;
Bourbon Street's loose jazz and sexy stomps;

the freaks and the fun for sale, where everything has to go;
the spicey smells and the trinkets tourists find;
the Mississippi's toy-boat sparkle show
as the city's patterned lights unpin behind.

Trolley-drinks are served as I leaf a magazine;
the next seat's eager to talk—a mini-chat
on what we're about, where going to or have been;
I wonder what each of the others could be at;

companions of the dark tubed in a silvered space
sealed like the tombs, disintegrating distance,
till we've humphered down to the taxied landing-place.
Relieved, we retrieve our luggage of our existence.

Mocking Bird Again

A bird we couldn't see
dropped song out of a tantalising tree,
not fashioning each individual note,
but imitating what it heard by rote.

Noting the copied sound,
we next day whistled at it from the ground;
but nothing answered. Tilting up to fly,
we saw it was a crow made no reply.

Could it be that birds find
a babel-language foreigning their kind
to baffle feathered signing, just as much
as we'd be, faced with Urdu or with Dutch?

London to Glasgow, First Class

He sits, a waist-up man with paper knees,
annoyed when someone passing drafts a breeze
that shifts his meaning's edge. Neat-coloured pens
angle his table. Figures are his friends,
white buttons on a calculator's face
whose totals always know their proper place.
Now and again his cellular 'phone rings:
we marvel at the urgent news it brings
from blurring towns the train goes rushing by;
an answer distance helps identify
to moiling managers he left behind
and who, despiting reason, always find
that on their best attentiveness he puts
his presence, cut like his expensive suits,
with confidence that profits out of loss,
and money recognises as its boss.

We unchauffeured, on whom his ways depend,
know we're the means to his rewarded end;
wonder what untouched satisfaction drives
his raw desire for fresh new-model wives;
what he can make that claims such public show?

Success that's only there when others know?

A Night on the Town

Streets that through daylight droned with thickened life
had eveninged into emptiness where, stark
as fame, strip-neon flared the dark
of London, drolled for pleasure and his wife.

Half-satisfied with fun's satiety,
couples twined arms, went linking off to bed.
Critics began to ponder what, when read,
might shake to-morrow's notoriety.

Voices dispersing happiness retreat,
stretching their distance on the frosted air,
leaving behind a mute discarded stare
of ragged shadow edging down the street

I knew that fellow, my companion said:
he could have credited both school and nation;
but, loosening resolve with vacillation,
he leafed the drift of circumstance instead.

I looked to where he nodded. Huddled bums
shuffled the arches; shadows of distress
so far subtracted into helplessness
the merest share of nothing made them chums.

They crumble into cartons, wrapped in smell
and rags stuck to the skin like a disease,
shifting their cramps to seek positioned ease,
each in his private vacancy of hell.

The last train's rumble runs along the bridge,
homing its crowds from theatres and dinners,
compartmenting success that warms the winners:
then silence shuts the night up like a fridge.

Unconfidential Clerk

He lives on in the memory of his friends.
the minister ritualled, sparsing thin relief
to sun-blenched mourning pews, the damp-stained walls
of dutiful piety, flaked with disbelief.

Even before they slid him to the furnace,
who remembered the contours of his face,
let alone the cast of his gestures, filling
the presence of his brief, domestic place?

Who can now conjure up his cornered smile,
the irrelevant voice success had never called
the odds on? Or the way his look deferred
whenever monied self-importance bawled?

He signed no words or music for the breath
of time to carry; strode no surface deed
for history to stultify, but served
the common dallyness of human need.

Glendaruel (1930–1990)

'Glendaruel, Glendaruel . . .'
Marjorie Kennedy-Fraser

Ancient hills harping the silence of legend,
a careless sun undoes the loosened shadows
that shawl your limbs, the misted sleep of darkness,
no longer Gaelic, shrouding you protection.

Such a place for a mythical bridal bed,
I used to think, uncertain how a woman
could spread herself upon a couch of mountains;
or what the shape of her wild progeny.

That day, the postmistress spoke about Cuchullain
and Deirdre as if it were only yesterday
naked word of them reached the rumoured ears
of the gods, like winds half-murmuring the grasses.

So once-upon-a-time there's no one certain
just when or how it happened; but their story
blows about this valley of changing seasons,
innocenced by children in their singing.

Now, a van from Dunoon delivers circulars;
hills, mists and trees mean what they always seemed,
only the river hesitates, passing the time of day,
forever here, forever time away.

All at Sea

Vandals have levered tombstones grassways, broken crosses,
causing distress to the cemetery attendants,
the papers say, though grey-veined hands of mosses
have long since scrawled anonymous amendments—

joiners, riveters, boiler-makers—men whose ships
cargoed the dignity of Clyde-built
from yards where weeds now fill the vacant slips
and crumbled basins fit-out only silt.

What urged the heaving vandals' shoulders? One in the eye
for fourteen billion years of uncaused cause?
The clenching of some question-fisted *Why*
against whatever system shares its flaws?

The glassy past's stare of inevitability,
its hulled-down certainties and fixed beliefs,
foundered in seas of incredulity,
though violence doesn't rub out history's griefs?

Respectful beds of flowers, a quilted lawn
above the threaded tunnels where the worms
bore through the hate and love they feed upon?
How can we measure wordless lack that turns

a man to fray the tie-ropes of his kind,
mooring in brittle voyaging to piers
of refuge fashioned by the human mind
from thrusts and pulls to which no tide adheres?

What use such questions blown against the wind
when -ologies and -isms each contend
meaningless answers doubt and death rescind?

Only forgiveness matters in the end.

Ah!

My muse, the bitch, has walked out on me;
gone, whoring after a younger lover,
leaving me only cold prose to fondle;
nothing to press to lyric orgasm;
only her absence, and the consternation
that never again she'll part her legs for me,
delight me, cry the mystery and pain.

Never again. . . .

VIII

French Mosquitoe's Woman: Selected Light Verse

A Scots Diversion
(based on a tale told to me by James Shaw Grant)

In sixteen hundred and eighty seven
    the Laird o Cona's bonnie dochter
gimp o the waist, brim fu o livan,
    hadnae a man, for nane had socht her.

Ae nicht the Laird, a wyce-like carle   *clever fellow*
    wha didna haud wi airs and graces,
speired at his wife, frae Dunimarle,   *questioned*
    whit way the lass micht show her paces.

Bessie, says he, nae suitor's near her;
    a barren stook's nae worth my name.
Hoo can we find a man tae steer her?   *rouse*
    She maun be made a married dame.

Seumas, says she, send doun tae Lunnon
    an order up a braw new spinet;
for oor gley Jean there'll be a run on,
    and mair than music soon be in it.

Her back'll airch and her heid haud steady;
    she'll show her guid points aa thegither
wi pose and posture o a leddy,
    the very image o her mither.

Bessie, says he, your Lawland smeddum's   *common sense*
    almost as shairp's my Hieland pride.
A bairn frae aff oor frostit maiden's
    heir tae my acres, gin I bide.

There dee'd in Lunnon Jock the Scraunter,
    a piper aince o bauld reknown,
what kittlt mair than bagpipe chaunter
    sae, banished, had frae Cona flown.

Jock and the spinet baith were kistit
    in brent-new boards the self-same day.
High tide fell past. Their vessel missed it,
    winds haen whoost up sic a frey.

Faur aff, on Cona, waefaced murners
   wha envied Jock's heroic deeds—
as guid a bunch o whisky-burners
   as ever glowed in dule-black weeds—

were bidean on the boat's arrival.
   To keep at bay fell Daith, the harrower
whisky's aye best for Man's survival:
   the streets grew narrower and narrower.

At last the boat blew roun the heidland
   and tied up at fair Cona's quay.
The Laird growled at his groom: *Mak speed, man.*
   Yon brand-new kist on deck's for me.

The mourners staggered tae the kirkyaird
   wi Jock on eight bent shouthers borne.
There never was sae keened a mirk caird   lamented a
   in aa the lush green lands of Lorn.   mournful fellow

Eight swayin ropes were strained tae sink him
   doun to his last eternal sleep.
Tak care, ain cried, *ye dinna dink him;*   jolt
   he'll be hard eneuch for earth to keep.

At that there rose a jingle-janglan
   as if the spheres lay deep i the grund
bagpipes and keyboards mingle-manglan,
   thirteen notes-warth o hellish sound.

Christ! cried the murners: *Jock's no deid yet.*
   Drappin his kist they flafft like hens
back to the bar wi tirlan heid, yet
   the likes o which nae sane man kens.

Up at the big hoose, Miss could barely
   wait till the boards were pressed asunder;
but the instrument she got sicht o fairly
   was puir Jock Scraunter's nine-day wonder.

Ae glimpse o that piper's silent chaunter
  gart Jeanie screich and faint clean awa.
'Twas a sicht, folk said, did so sairly daunt her
  she vowed she'd never be mairrit an aa.

Ye Hieland lairds, gin you've daughters wha lack men
  let them gang whatever gait they may,
for ye canna be sure hoo music'll tak them
  whatever kind o a piper ye pay.

Ballad of the Hare and the Bassethound
(for my grandchildren)

The bassethound's a mournful fellow;
long ears that trail along the ground,
a baying voice that's like a cello,
a tail that circles round and round.

Yet bassethounds were bred for chasing,
through France's royal days of old,
the breathless hare, at first outpacing
the hound who, once he snuffed a hold

of the hare's scent, kept slowly clumbering
ditches, branches, burns and fields
till at the end of all his lumbering,
the limping hare, spring broken, yields.

We're civilised. So basset Billy,
his snuffling anchored to the ground,
was amiable, harmless, silly,
seeking for things he never found.

One sudden day he bumped his snout on
a lump of fur, a sleeping hare.
Poor Billy gazed with wrinkled doubt on
the creature that returned his stare.

At once the hare sent distance arcing
as towards the setting sun he sped,
while Billy sat upon his barking,
then turned and oppositely fled.

But not for long. The old blood-royal
that courses through a basset's veins
is not a thing for time to spoil,
even when it feeds slow-thinking brains.

His massive paws he pushed before him
and slithered to a skidding halt.
In vain did I command, implore him—
ancestral blood cried out 'Assault!'

So yelping ancient doggy noises,
Billy set off in late pursuit.
Time waits for no such equiposes:
the jinking hare by then had put

two lengthy fields from where he started
and, smalling, breached a hill's horizon,
Billy, essentially kind-hearted,
pulled up with innocent surprise on

his wrinkled features. Body wagging,
he ambled back to where I waited.
With asking eyes he lay there sagging,
face saved and old French honour sated;

as if to say: 'Come on now, praise me
for showing sense; en Français, *sens*;
like you, to kill's a thought dismays me,
so *honi soit qui mal y pense!*'

The French Mosquitoes' Woman

There comes a moment in the fate of nations
when even politicians can't dissemble,
as history prepares its future stations,
and human kind's great forward leaps assemble.
Scotland the Brave (oh stars and planets, tremble!),
a land that thinks the world's a football pitch
and truth the thing her players most resemble,
was stricken by a dire infectious itch,
attracted, folk said, by 'a stuck-up foreign bitch!'

A wealthy Scot had wedded to his person
a Londoner, patrician by extraction,
making a Cholmondeley into a Macpherson,
a change that might have seemed a poor subtraction
had she not 'leaderened' each local faction
of politics and charity. So queenly
her talent to devise a course of action
all shadowed disagreement melted cleanly
leaving dull shame, which her opponents felt most keenly.

The flesh of healthy Scots is tough and leathery,
just like their wit and thirst. The wise explain
this comes from striding mountains damp and heathery,
the breeding ground of midges, Scotland's bane
that causes foreign tourists clouds of pain
yet leaves the natives more or less unscarted,
with energy to brace against the strain
of make-believing nationhood, great-hearted
with pride for what they've not yet noticed long-departed.

Hortensia Macpherson (née Miss Cholmondeley),
despite the way her jaw pronounced decision,
had soft and tender skin, however rumly
this seemed to those who'd cleft before her vision.
Although her will held midges in derision,
blown from their flight-path by a freakish storm
down on her garden buzzed an armed division
of French mosquitoes fiercer than the norm
intent on finding flesh on which they might perform.

Their poisoned lances in Hortensia's features
caused such indignity of face and mind
she bought a recent treatise on the creatures
and, reading, was delighted there to find
the havoc all the work of just one kind;
female mosquitoes duly impregnated.
While sex was not for English girls designed
(such Continental vice she simply hated!),
what harm in getting female insects satiated?

She wired to Oxford for a man so brainy
nothing existed he could not invent.
As, freshly slept, from the long-distance train, he
alighted, like a pop-star he'd been 'sent'.
Already, squiggled calculations rent
whole reams of paper. There had never been
such learning to a simple problem bent.
Quickly he built what none had ever seen,
an electronic male-attracting noise machine.

The first time this contraption was in motion,
midges and male mosquitoes set upon
their females. Swathed in sun-protecting lotion,
Hortensia found peace upon her lawn.
From sunrise through to dusk, then round to dawn,
ripped female insects fell to earth in pieces.
Lured by the soft machine, fresh males were drawn,
as fathers fought for daughters, uncles nieces;
to countless millions ran a single day's deceases.

One careless hour, when walking forth in Crail,
a geriatric pedalling a tricycle
knocked down the don, in health but spare and frail,
and left him thinned and cooling like an icicle.
Hortensia arrived upon her bicycle—
she'd left her breakfast urgently to find him
before she'd time to savour her first Ricicle—
suddenly anxious, eager to remind him
to sign a maintenance contract that would fully bind him.

Awakening, she'd dreamt the sound had faltered,
her sleeping ear had heard a distant roar.
Once home, she found indeed the pitch had altered;
a hundred lustful dogs besieged her door.
She fought her way inside, and with an oar,
four skis, a shooting stick, and what lay handy
she mustered all the courage that she bore
to build a barricade, then turned to Mandy,
her neutered bitch, and asked: *What makes these brutes so randy?*

Before the dog could answer with the *woof*
it used for all such questions, awful shaking
broke out, and rocked the house from floor to roof.
A herd of bulls had set the garden quaking,
while sweating, rampant stallions started raking
up trees and bushes as with cloven hoof.
Hortensia felt new measures needed taking—
the damage done was quite sufficient proof.
She rang the police. The law could not remain aloof.

She'd made the GPO have all lines buried
for conservation reasons. The upholder
of British rule, though rarely to be hurried,
at once picked up his 'phone, and promptly told her
of what he, too, was an amazed beholder.
The zoo was loose, and elephants were trumpeting,
pulling church steeples down. Insanely bolder,
lions were chasing cows, obscenely rumpeting,
while even he might not refuse some tasty crumpeting!

What happened next? I hesitate to tell you;
but news is a self-propagating carrier
the media just package up and sell you.
To predatory man, the world's worst harrier,
skis, shooting-stick and oars proved little barrier.
Hortensia, in bed a chilling shoulder,
at last learned what it meant for man to parry her,
though not Macpherson. Scarce a second older,
and there was not a virgin left for age to moulder.

Like most good Scots, Macpherson, down in London
seeking his fortune, suffered grief and pain
learning from chat-shows how his wife was undone.
Yet, he reflected, loss may turn to gain.
This public madness must be rendered sane
before he could attempt denied felicity.
He hailed a taxi, drove to Pudding Lane
and reached the Central Board of Electricity
who listened to his plans and promised their complicity.

A switch was thrown. Hush fell across the country.
Industry droned to stillness. Darkness spread.
Trade Union leaders shook the hands of gentry,
both humanised through sharing common dread.
Meanwhile, a local handyman called Ned
went crawling to the source of the disaster
(averting passing gaze from madam's bed,
according to instructions from his master)
and smashed the noise machine with blows first quick, then
    faster.

Somewhere in London, Mrs Cherry Whitemouse
claimed licensed television was to blame
for all the trouble. Self-erected lighthouse,
she flashed out moral protest at the shame
this Scots contagion smeared on England's name.
The Attorney General declared the facts seemed
too vague for prosecution all the same.
Snorting of how protective secret pacts beamed,
the puny private Whitemouse prosecution axe gleamed.

There's some might think we now should draw a veil,
though tougher things than veils were rent asunder.
Macpherson, worn with joy, grew thin and pale;
six feet of his own earth he soon lay under.
Hortensia, enraptured by the wonder
of what she'd dubbed 'the Continental vice',
repented of her electronic blunder
tied five times more the matrimonial splice
while Cherry Whitemouse slept, embalmed in sugared ice.

Scots readers always feel a moral ending
essential to a tale like this, uplifting.
So let us try. Say, life's too short for spending
thought's effort on the riskiness of shifting
Nature's accustomed balance. As for rifting
whatever lute strikes chords that sound offences
to narrow ears, then innocence goes drifting
towards chaos and what censorship dispenses.
Say also, laughter harmonises jangled senses.

The Bridal Consultant

The Bridal Consultant Miss Honey Hymen
importantly pranced to her virgin's window.
The traffic had jammed. As she flashed a neat thigh, men
sat watching her fumble discreetly to undo
the zip at the back of a white wedding dress,
cocking her hand in a genteel caress.

Miss Hymen was fifty and chestless. Her dummy
had more of the natural feminine shape:
it angled its knees, it stuck out its tummy,
it pointed its fingers the better to drape
the yards of material used in the setting
that customers knew just how much they were getting.

The dress didn't budge from those elegant shoulders,
so Hymen indulged in a lady-like wrench;
but the virtuous dummy, unyielding, was cold as
a country resister upon a park bench.
In vain did the arm of La Hymen cajole;
the creature resisted erect as a pole.

She thrust her right leg to the dummy's bent left one,
as if she'd embarked on a *thé dansant valse*;
the feet of the creature proceeded to drift on
the shift of its fabric, misleadingly false:
a hand to its neck, a wrist to its . . . ooch!
Miss Hymen resembled a Lesbian butch.

She tramped on its toes with a smile to dissemble,
and levered the dummy back onto its pins.
But a glance at those men set her knees all a-tremble,
as they sat in their cars on the breadth of their grins.
With a no-nonsense grip she forced up its palms,
and fell to the floor holding two severed arms.

At once the white dress slithered off the bare torso,
collapsing its shape on the fallen Miss Hymen
such disgrace brought a blush to her face; all the more so
in front of an ogle of double-glazed wry men;
but swiftly the orgy was brought to its ending,
the lights turning green and a dust-sheet descending.

A Report on the Coroner's Inquest on the Late Don Giovanni

Upon a time—we can't allow the fairy-tale
suspension of our disbelief to soften
into traditional *Once*, or we would truly fail
our public duty, for it happens often,
though not in such exaggerated measure,
when men pursue the thought of endless pleasure.

By any standards, an unusual case:
no body: not even a heap of charred bones.
Only a burn-marked hole in the ground, and the face
of disbelief, as they set down warning cones
so that no one accidentally should tumble
into the place that gave the fatal rumble.

First question. Just what exactly occurred?
A clomping statue, the servant said, appeared
from the adjacent graveyard. A grim scowl slurred
the frozen features of the once-revered
Commandant, killed duelling one who fled,
discovered attacking a daughter in her bed.

Though it's difficult to piece together the bits
of what followed next—Leporello under the table,
frightened out of his less than steady wits—
we must search for truth as best as we are able;
the servant told to invite the statue to dine
while the master quaffed a glass of his vintage wine.

It appears that the statue called on the Don to repent,
but he, not unnaturally, placed great reliance
on the fact that graveyard memorials aren't meant
to step from their fixities and utter defiance.
Caught in a clench so cold he could hardly yell
blue murder, the Don, astonished, was dragged to Hell;

a place the location of which remains unknown
to earthly cartographers—though not, it seems,
back safely on his plinth, to the man of stone.
Was it all hallucination? The boozy dreams
of a too-rich meal? Or, as the gasman claims,
an explosion brought about by a leak in the mains?

You might justly claim that the servant suffered a touch
of madness, brought about by frequent excess,
against which, he says, he protested; though not too much,
being forced at swordpoint to put on the dress
of his master, stay behind to deflect the blame
and be dubbed half-guilty of a double shame.

There were tradesmen's reports by masons and morticians,
claiming cement and grass were alike intact;
and a promise by the local politicians
to 'catch the guilty party'; and, in on the act,
MP's condemning 'this gruesome vigilante
who'd behaved like something out of the pages of Dante.'

Witnesses on camels, donkeys, planes—
France's two hundred, Germany's hundred-and-one,
ninety-three Turkey's, a thousand and twenty Spain's
sixty-four Italy's—claiming they'd been undone;
women of every rank and shape and age,
nurturing the fulfilment of spent rage.

It wasn't so much the persistence and urbanity
with which the Don had pursued his repeated aim
of spreading females underneath his vanity
as the restless, resistless speed with which they became
his sexual fodder; nubile, warm or tough,
all were the same to him, refined or rough.

He'd had, he claims, a domineering mother
with whom he was ambiguously related;
to other men he felt more than a brother,
except when strings of women kept him sated:
though practice hones the lover's pleasing skill,
the self he knew could only fear its fill.

Readers, we won't use up your time retelling
what twice a thousand witnesses reported;
some had been left with virgin bellies swelling,
others yielded before the petting started:
the strange thing was, their attitudes were ambivalent—
they had never known a lover his equivalent—

nor trouble you with the brats called Giovanni
that peopled Europe (they are still being born)
from Gothenburg to Rome, or Zakopane;
none, we're assured, is languishing forlorn,
the pleasure that their mothers had conceiving
in some way mitigating Dad's deceiving.

Women whose minds were mushed by sweet Romances,
bored with their marriage—'Is that all there's to it?'—
found that in bed variety enhances,
inviting window-cleaners in to do it;
for them, this passing Don they'd never schemed for
exploded pleasures that they'd had to dream for.

But retrospectively, respectability
means keeping on the clothing of convention,
if we would earn this facile world's civility
that's held together by such social tension;
protesting much, they couldn't quite conceal
a satisfaction somehow more than real.

The funny thing is, none expressed disgust
as at a rapist, fearing his infection;
only a lulled suspending wave of trust
that broke on the experience of perfection;
the kind of unreal thing, larger than life,
you don't discover as a routined wife.

Last to appear were the women closest to him,
recently shocked, with nothing left to hide.
Donna Elvira, who designed to woo him,
surrendering when he'd sworn she'd be his bride;
who, finding he'd deserted her, repented,
and in a convent from her herself absented.

Zerlina, so enraptured by his dancing,
who had only meant to make her husband jealous—
a shadowy squeeze, a bit of bosom-glancing—
felt with alarm the speedy Don grow zealous,
so screamed aloud when he began his skirting
beyond the outward decencies of flirting.

And Donna Anna, frigid, undersexed,
who'd fought the assailant off—though no one knew,
not even the dummy husband whom she'd vexed
by holding back her love, could swear it was true—
seemed set to become a dominant virgin matron
of a kind that countless charities get as patron.

He might have got away with it for ever
had he not slipped his guard enough to go for
that domineering woman, so unclever
the passing years had left her little to show for;
though killing her old father in a duel
was legal, spells are broken when we're cruel.

Whatever myth that down the years he carried
that pleasured women of all creeds and sizes,
deserted him the moment that he parried
the Commandant's defence. You don't win prizes
by letting anger commandeer your mood
and leaving your opponent cooled in blood.

What did he seek? The question keeps arising.
Was he the basic spirit of desire,
gene-faulted? Or just macho-fantasising
the Guinness Book of Records might inspire
to gain unusual entry? He's immortal,
a threatening legend lingering round love's portal.

The Coroner, aware of his critics waiting
beside those gutters running tabloid ink
to accuse him of dubious taste, and suggest castrating
a fitting punishment (were it not that the brink
of Hell had apparently swallowed the victim whole)
left God to be his judge. If the man had a soul,

whatever that might be, he'd face a reckoning
for his crimes if (the duel apart) that's what they were.
Seeing hypocrisy all around him beckoning,
the deliberate coroner came at last to aver
an open verdict, which the upright opposed
in a case that, in point of fact, could never be closed.

Brevities

I DIETARY

There once was a girl from Cologne
couldn't leave Kölnisch Wasser alone;
   for breakfast, lunch, dinner
    she drank it, grew thinner,
then vaporised down to the bone.

II CHILDLESS

Little doggie, eat your beefies
and I'll take you for a walkies;
then a bone to clean your teefhies—
pity that we can't have talkies.

III PRIORITIES

Convoked upon their supernatural probes,
Is't Thee or You the Lord prefers when praying?
rustles the hierarchical silken robes,
forgetting that those words they have us saying
were made by man to minimise despairing.
If doubtful God exists, would He be caring?

IV THE JUDGEMENT

I want it both ways, the salesman said:
you here at home, her there in bed.
So she picked up an axe and cleavered his head.

The prosecution urged she was bad,
the defending counsel claimed she was mad;
as for herself, she thought she'd been had.

How can you face two ways, for a start?
She had merely fitted him out for the part
with a biblical stroke of King Solomon's art.

V   DOCTORS WHO PROPOSED A PUNITIVE TAX ON CIGARETTES

Pile tax on fags? Doctors, you take the breath
away! You think our Chancellor a chancer?
Deny the poor the right to early death
as Fellows of the Friendship of Lung Cancer?

VI   BURNS IN ELYSIUM

Move over Burns. Your long ordeal is done:
MacDiarmid scholarship has just begun.

VII   AH WELL!

Should I be cremated, or not?, a man
of God and Hypochondria was musing.
Crossing the road, a sausage-maker's van
relieved him of the agony of choosing.

VIII   GLASGOW TO THE PLAY

Nae mair muckt-oot kailyairds, or smooch-in Hielan glens;
its pubs an bets oan fitba, beatan the kids an wife,
the flash o a broken bottle the drama a he-man kens.
The warld dusnae think it 'significant'? Then the world's oot o
    touch wi Life.

IX   TO CATCH THE LAST POST

The party's almost over. Though at times a trifle odd,
I've thoroughly enjoyed it. Thank you for having me, God.

X   A SORT OF PRAYER, PERHAPS

As time undoes me for the grave,
dear God, from your supposed Hereafter,
an unbeliever's boon I crave—
let what goes last from me be laughter!

Notes

p. 81 **'Responsibilities'**
For those unfamiliar with the story of Beethoven's opera *Fidelio*, the following note may help in the understanding of this poem. Florestan has been imprisoned in a fortress near Seville for political reasons by Pizzaro, who puts about news of his captive's death. Florestan's wife, Leonora, discovers her husband's whereabouts and in the guise of a young man called Fidelio gets taken on by the jailer, who has refused to murder her husband as ordered by Pizzaro. When Pizzaro learns that the Minister of State is about to inspect the fortress, he again orders the jailer to murder Florestan. Pizzaro then draws a dagger to do the deed himself, but Fidelio throws off her disguise and holds him back at pistol point. A distant trumpet announces the impending arrival of the Minister, who frees his old friend Florestan and has Pizzaro arrested.

p. 87 **'To Hugh MacDiarmid'**
Though most of the causes Hugh MacDiarmid espoused have proved false trails to nowhere—social credit, the inevitability of Communism, the resurgence of Scots and Gaelic—by questioning every accepted Scottish value he did, for a time, appear to have changed our 'climate of the mind', though whether or not permanently, I am now much less sure.

p. 121 **'A Net to Catch the Winds'**
STANZA 5 Sir Compton Mackenzie claimed to have the gift of total recall from the age of two. His autobiographical *Octaves* abound in examples. In October 1947 he came to lunch with my wife and me, along with C M Grieve ('Hugh MacDiarmid'), Professor John Glaister, the forensic expert, and the Reverend H S Maclelland, the actor-manqué minister of Trinity Church (now the Henry Wood SNO Centre) in Claremont Street. My wife elected to serve fish, but a storm at sea had delayed deliveries to the shops. During the soup course, while my wife was trying to advance things in the kitchen, Mackenzie, deep in anecdotal reminiscence, picked up the fish server instead of his spoon and plunged it into the soup. Soup spattered in all directions through the decorative holes. 'Ah! A social error,' said Mackenzie, wiping the server on his napkin, and picking up his story in mid-sentence.

More than thirty years later, in conversation with my wife, he recalled the occasion, the trivial incident and the exact details of the location of our flat in Southpark Avenue, Glasgow, to which this was his only visit.

STANZA 29 MacDiarmid publicly supported the Russian armed interventions in Hungary and Czechoslovakia, acts of aggression that disgusted the Free World.

STANZA 30 Sadly, the Scots tongue has steadily declined under the relentless pressures of cinema, radio and television. While it has certainly been a long time in dying, the erosion of its individual words, leaving behind only English words pronounced in a dialect manner, does not augur well for its future as a fruitful medium for creative writing.

STANZA 72 Nicholas Fairbairn, QC, whose original and colourful garb and forthright opinions made him a noted figure even before he became a Member of Parliament and in Mrs Thatcher's Government Solicitor General for Scotland. In *Thomas Campion: Poet, Composer and Physician* (1970), Lowbury, Salter and Young remark: 'In contrast with the Renaissance ideal of the balanced man who aspired to do all things well, the ideal cultivated in the nineteenth and twentieth centuries has been specialist and monolithic; hence a distrust of the varied talents of the "Jack-of-all-trades".'

STANZA 77 See Edwin Morgan's poem 'An Addition to the Family'. Although the poet got to know my basset-hound, Hector (and Toby, his successor), the story of my double interest in basset-horns and basset-hounds, the basis of the poem, was told to Morgan by George Bruce before Morgan met the animal.

STANZA 79 At the Edinburgh International Festival and the Three Choirs Festival.

STANZA 80 The reference to Sir Karl Popper's theory (in *Unended Quest*) that great art exists in 'world 3' as distinct from things ('world 1') or our subjective interpretation of them ('world 2').

STANZA 81 Francis George Scott was not only the English teacher of the boy C M Grieve (Hugh MacDiarmid) at a Langholm school, but a perceptive and instructive critic to many late Scots poets. (c.f. my *Francis George Scott and the Scottish Renaissance* [1980].)

STANZA 106 'piecemeal social engineering'. The phrase is Popper's.

STANZA 120 Lorn MacIntyre, Alan Bold, Duncan Glen and Tom Scott (towards none of whom I bear any malice), whose many letters to *The Scotsman* have included the suggestion that Hugh MacDiarmid might be commemorated by the establishment of a Bardic College.

p. 223 **'A Wedding'**
The portraits in this sonnet sequence, while drawn from the life, come from several wedding parties. They are what the brothers of the Trade Union Congress might call 'composites'. Consequently, they do not portray any actual persons, living or dead.

p. 239 **'A Scots Divertimento'**
Travelling around the Highlands more than two decades ago to judge a schools environmental award with the playwright and newspaperman James Shaw Grant (later to become Chairman of the Crofters' Commission), my companion regaled me with a tale of mistaken luggage identity which befell a much respected nineteenth century Gaelic-speaking minister. That the tale aroused in my mind rather more robust comic possibilities is in no way the fault of Mr Grant.

p. 248 **'A Report on the Coroner's Inquest on the Late Don Giovanni'**
The character of the irresistible seducer Don Giovanni Tenorio was probably created by Tirso de Molina (1571–1641) in his play *El Burlador de Sevilla*. Amongst those to elaborate on his exploits have been Thomas Shadwell (*The Libertine*, 1676), Carlo Goldeni (*Don Giovanni Tenorio o sia Il Dissoluto*, 1736) and the opera composer Guissepe Gazzaniga, for whom in 1787 a libretto of the libertine's exploits was provided by Giovanni Bertati. This opera book was probably known to Lorenzo da Ponte, who may have suggested it to Mozart as a subject for the opera he was commissioned in that year to write for Prague. While Da Ponte vastly improved on his predecessor's work, he did borrow from it heavily.

It is the death of the Mozart/Da Ponte Don that is the subject of my poem. Don Giovanni, having successfully seduced hundreds of women all over Europe, is repulsed by Donna Anna, the daughter of the Commendatore, who thereupon engages the Don in a duel in which the older man is killed. Donna Anna is in due course comforted by her somewhat characterless fiancee Don Ottavio, whom she apparently holds sexually at arm's length. Donna Elvira, whom the Don has seduced by promising marriage, but deserted, teams up with Donna Anna and Don Ottavio to prevent Giovanni seducing Zerlina, the pert fiance of the peasant Masetto. Foiled again, and defying all suggestions that he repent, the Don sits down to supper attended by his servant, Leporello, who has been a reluctant accomplice in the Don's exploits. Elvira arrives to make a final vain plea for Giovanni to repent. As she leaves, she shrieks with terror. Leporello, sent to find out the cause, reports that the statue of the Commendatore is outside. Leporello is told to invite the statue to supper. The statue stomps in, invites the Don to sup with him, takes the Don's hand and together they disappear into a fiery pit.